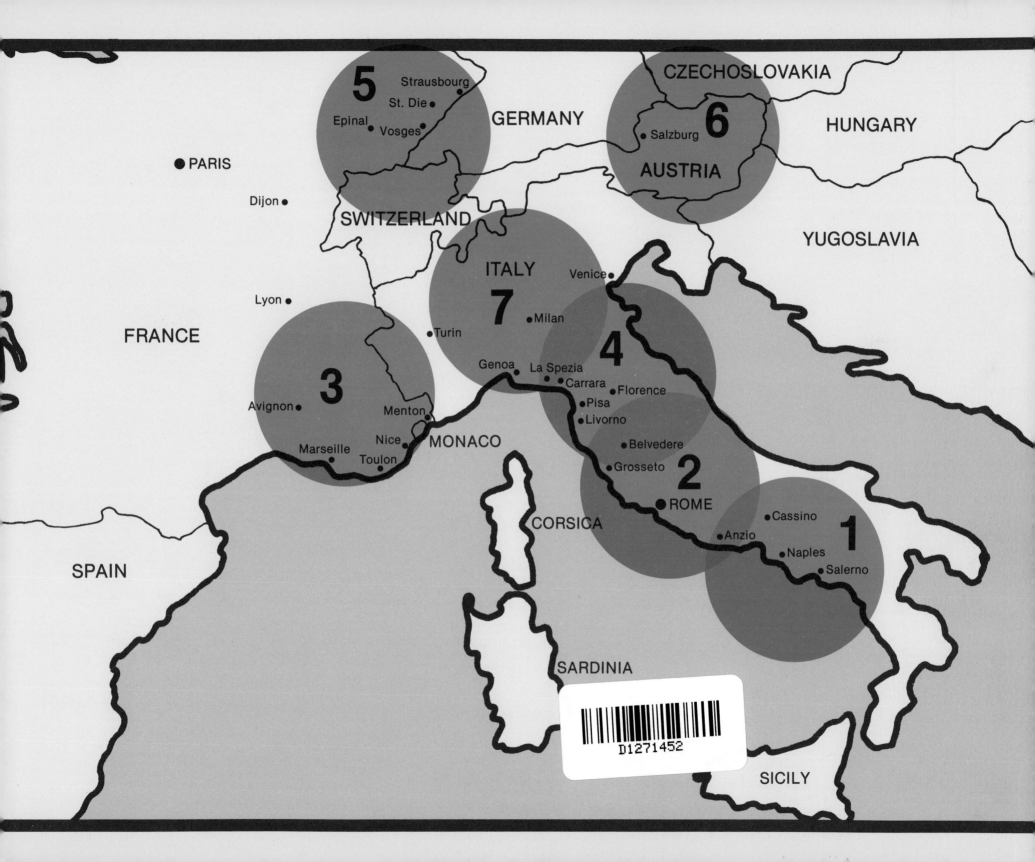

GO FOR BROKE

A Pictorial History of the Japanese American
100th Infantry Battalion and the 442d Regimental Combat Team

By
Chester Tanaka

Go For Broke, Inc.
Richmond, California

EDITORIAL BOARD: *Col (ret) James M. Hanley, Capt (ret) Richard K. Hayashi, Harry Iwafuchi, Maj (ret) Tom Kawaguchi, Col (ret) Young O. Kim, Col (ret) Tom Kobayashi, Eric Saul, and Maj (ret) Orville C. Shirey.*

GRAPHICS: *Tatsumi Iwate, jacket design; Chester Tanaka, book design and production.*

Library of Congress Cataloging in Publication Data

By Chester Tanaka

Go For Broke:
A Pictorial History of the 100/442d Regimental Combat Team

Catalog Card Number: 81-84167

Published by
Go For Broke, Inc.
Richmond, California

Distributed by
JACP, Inc.
414 East Third Avenue
San Mateo, California 94401

Printed and bound in the United States of America
by Turner Printing Company, Oakland, California

Dedication

We do not intend with this book to glorify war, to declare that "might makes right," or simply to pay lip-service to our honored dead. In these pages we offer our unending thanks to those who gave their all and to the loved ones they left behind. We pay homage to those who made the numbers "100" and "442" meaningful and sacred with their lives. We are inspired once again by their battle cry for life, "Go for Broke"! And they achieved this in a time of utter uncertainty, frustration, and degradation. Through this dark chaos, each of them took the giant step forward and upward, giving new meaning to liberty, justice, and human rights. And, in the course of their giving and serving, they died before they could see and taste the fruits of their sacrificial labors. They were mostly young men who had their future before them. They were ordinary youths wanting to live, but they became "extraordinary" as they dared to choose to come forth from the concentration camps to fight for the land that had incarcerated them and their families. And they became heroes because they dared to take that first step to become "equals" with others in American society. They stood apart and were not dismayed or dissuaded by forces that weighed against them.

And we know that they sincerely desired to return home when their work was done. But they died, not in their homeland in beds of comfort, but alone, in agony, in a strange land . . . ignorant of the legacy that their passing would create.

Somewhere deep inside each of them they must have known that "it is better to fail in a cause that will ultimately succeed" than to "succeed in a cause that will ultimately fail." They attained the stature of giants as they fought and secured human rights, justice, and equality not only for themselves and their families but for all who were oppressed.

It is in memory and homage to these gallant officers and men of the 100th Infantry Battalion and the 442d Regimental Combat Team that this book is dedicated.

CAPT (CHAPLAIN) GEORGE AKI
100/442d REGIMENTAL COMBAT TEAM

100th Infantry Battalion

Headquarters Company
A Company
B Company
C Company
D Company
E Company
F Company
Medical Detachment

442d Regimental Combat Team

Headquarters Company
Anti-tank Company
Cannon Company
Medical Detachment
Service Company

100th Battalion	*2d Battalion*	*3d Battalion*
Headquarters Company	Headquarters Company	Headquarters Company
A Company	E Company	I Company
B Company	F Company	K Company
C Company	G Company	L Company
D Company	H Company	M Company

522d Field Artillery Battalion

Headquarters Battery
A Battery
B Battery
C Battery
Service Battery and Medical Detachment

232d Combat Engineer Company

206th Army Band

Author's Note

The men and units whose achievements are described in this narrative are representative rather than all-inclusive. We would have liked to include the stories of all of the men who earned the Distinguished Service Crosses, Silver Stars, Bronze Stars, and other decorations, and the stories of how the units earned their citations and awards, but the limitations of time and space have rendered this approach impossible. We sincerely regret that full coverage in the narrative or in the listings could not be given and we ask your understanding in this matter.

Confronted with over 4,000 photographs, the Editorial Board spent weeks culling and sorting to reduce this number to a manageable 300. This was still 100 more than the space allocated. Finally after several more eye-blurring and hair-tearing sessions, the Board sifted this number down to 240 photographs, 8 maps, and 2 endpapers — we think.

The editorial "we" is quite apropos here. This publication is truly a team effort.

Eric Saul, curator of the Presidio Army Museum, San Francisco, personally conducted an oral history program among the officers and men of the 100/442. He, somehow, elicited accounts and insights that, in many cases, the veterans had never told their wives or children. Needless to say, his contribution was invaluable.

Another stalwart was Tom Kawaguchi, who unflaggingly nurtured, endorsed, and encouraged the telling of this story. In addition, he skillfully steered the publication through numerous administrative and financial shoals. In four words — no Tom, no book!

A great debt also is owed to Maj (ret) Orville C. Shirey, Regimental S-2 Officer. Maj Shirey wrote and edited the original history of the unit, the *442d Combat Team,* which was printed and published in Italy by MTOUSA (Mediterranean Theater of Operations, U.S. Army) in 1945. Upon returning to Washington, D.C., he expanded on his earlier work and produced the now standard and classic volume, *Americans: The Story of the 442d Combat Team.* These books became the source for almost all the other histories and were certainly so for this pictorial version.

Endless letters, phone calls, and meetings have honed and produced this final manuscript. What is truly good came from the officers and men, the oral history interviewees, and the patient editors and reviewers. The rest is mine — from personal recollection, reading, and research.

We welcome your comments, your criticisms, and your corrections and will incorporate as many as possible in subsequent editions.

We enjoyed producing this book and hope you find it worthy of your waiting and trust.

Chester Tanaka
April 1982

The Distinguished Service Cross

The Distinguished Service Cross is the Nation's highest award for military valor following the Congressional Medal of Honor. Fifty-two* members of the 100/442d Regimental Combat Team have earned this medal of great military distinction — 51 are listed here, alphabetically with rank and unit as of time of action († indicates killed in action, †† missing in action.)

Irving H. Akahoshi, PFC: 100th/Hq Co
Henry Y. Arao, S/Sgt: 100th/Co A
Masao Awakuni, Pvt: 100th/Co C
Yoshimi R. Fujiwara, S/Sgt: 2d Bn/Co G
Barney F. Hajiro, PFC: 3d Bn/Co I
† Mikio Hasemoto, Pvt: 100th/Co B
† Joe Hayashi, Pvt: 3d Bn/Co K
Shizuya Hayashi, Pvt: 100th/Co A
Jesse M. Hirata, Pvt: 100th/Co B
George S. Iida, T/Sgt: 2d Bn/Co G
Daniel K. Inouye, 1st Lt: 2d Bn/Co E
Young O. Kim, Capt: 100th/Co B
Yeiki Kobashigawa, 2d Lt: 100th/Co B
† Kiichi Koda, PFC: 100th/Co A
Haruto Kuroda, PFC: 100th/Co B
† Robert T. Kuroda, S/Sgt: 2d Bn/Co E
† Harry F. Madakoro, PFC: 3d Bn/Co K
† Kazuo Masuda, S/Sgt: 2d Bn/Co F
Shinyei Matayoshi, T/Sgt: 2d Bn/Co G
Fujio Miyamoto, S/Sgt: 3d Bn/Co K
Takeichi Miyashiro, 1st Lt: 100th/Co C
Kaoru Moto, PFC: 100th/Co C
† Kiyoshi K. Muranaga, PFC: 2d Bn/Co F
† Hiroshi Nagami, Sgt: 2d Bn/Co F
Masato Nakae, PFC: 100th/Co A
† Shinyei Nakamine, Pvt: 100th/Co B
† William K. Nakamura, PFC: 2d Bn/Co G
† Robert K. Nakasaki, Sgt: 100th/Co A
Joe M. Nishimoto, PFC: 2d Bn/Co G

Distinguished Service Cross

"For extraordinary heroism in connection with a military operation against an armed enemy"

Allan M. Ohata, 1st Lt: 100th/Co B
Yukio Okutsu, T/Sgt: 2d Bn/Co F
Frank H. Ono, PFC: 2d Bn/Co G
Thomas Y. Ono, Pvt: 100th/Co B
† Masano Otake, 2d Lt: 100th/Co C
† Kazuo Otani, S/Sgt: 2d Bn/Co G
†† Itsumu Sasaoka, S/Sgt: 100th/Co A
Manabu Suehiro, Cpl: 100th/Co A
† Togo S. Sugiyama, Sgt: 2d Bn/Co H
Tsuneo Takemoto, T/Sgt: 2d Bn/Co E
Yukio Takaki, PFC: 100th/Co B
† Ronald K. Takara, Sgt: 100th/Co B
† Joe S. Takata, Sgt: 100th/Co B
† Larry T. Tanimoto, Sgt: 3d Bn/Co I
† Ted T. Tanouye, T/Sgt: 3d Bn/Co K
Jim Y. Tazoi, PFC: 3d Bn/Co K
† Thomas I. Yamanaga, PFC: 100th/Co A
† Gordon K. Yamashiro, S/Sgt: 3d Bn/Co K
† Fred S. Yasuda, PFC: 3d Bn/Co K
Hiroshi R. Yasutake, PFC: 100th/Co C
† Masuichi Yogi, PFC: 3d Bn/Co K
Yukio Yokota, T/Sgt: 100th/Co B

* According to Gen Jacob L. Devers, former Chief of Army Field Forces, 52 Distinguished Service Crosses were awarded to the 100/442 (Adj Gen Office). Inquiry as to identity, action, place, company, and rank has been made but information was not available at press time. We apologize for omissions and misspellings that may have occurred in this edition.

Acknowledgments

The author gratefully acknowledges that without the generous assistance and support of the Editorial Board and the scores of veterans who donated or shared their photographs and album collections, and who gave so freely of themselves in the oral history and personal interviews, this book would never have been written.

We wish to thank the following contributors: Yasuo Abiko, Kenichi Akagi, Kathryn S. Box, Brian Buhl, Hung Wai Ching, Gen Mark W. Clark, Robert K. Combs, Fred Dobana, Shigeyuki Doi, Yoshio Doi, John C. Elstead, Mansaku "Monte" Fujita, Col Mitsuyoshi Fukuda, June and Tak Goto, J. Edward Green, Harry Hamada, Jerry Hashimoto, Carole Hayashino-Kagawa, Col (Chaplain) Hiroshi Higuchi*, Hiro Hirano, Louis M. Hirata*, Harry Honda, Mas Hongo, Hiroshi Hori, Albert Ichihara, Duncan Ikezoe, Ichiro Imamura, Howard Imazeki, James G. Inafuku, Senator Daniel K. Inouye, Susumu Ito, Hideo Kajikawa, Shozo Kajioka, Col Jimmie Kanaya, Ken Kaneko, Lt Col (ret) Robert Katayama, Alexander A. Kauhini, James Kawakami, Capt Norman Kurlan, Mits Kojimoto, Lt Col James Lovell, Jim Makino, Buddy Mamiya, Mike M. Masaoka, Tad Masaoka, Tom Masamori, Roy Matsuda, Cal Matsumoto, Senator Masayuki "Spark" Matsunaga, Col Virgil R. Miller, Jr., Maj Ted Miyagishima, George Miyahara, Mitch Miyamoto, Shigeru Miyamoto, Hiroshi Miyamura, Jeff Mori, Art Morimitsu, Joe H. Nagaki, Katsuji Nakamura, Shigeru "Kelly" Nakamura, Lyle Nelson, Raymond Nosaka, Wally Nunotani, Lt Col William Oda, Richard S. Oguro, George Oiye, 2d Lt Ichiro Okada, Toshio M. Okamura, Jimmy Oshiro, Kazuma Oyama, Col Henry Oyasato, D.C. Pence, Mitch Postel, Haru Sakaji, Daisy Satoda, Dr. Hiroshi "Joe" Shimamura, Goro Sumida, Tom Takahashi, Maj Michio Takata, Hiroshi Takusagawa, Edward Tamanaha, Joseph K. Tanaka, John Tateishi, Rudy Tokiwa, Junior Uranaka, Gene Uratsu, Len Wilkerson, Henry S. Yamada, George Yamamoto, "Fuzzy" Yoshimasu, and Florence Yoshiwara. "Da Boys" of the 100th Infantry Battalion (Separate), "Da Boys" of the 442d Regimental Combat Team, The Fort Point and Army Museum Association, The Presidio Army Museum, and The 100/442/MIS Museum Foundation.

We also wish to express our special thanks to the following persons: Editor, Masako Tanaka; Associate Editors—Sandra Fulmer, Richard K. Hayashi, Tom Kawaguchi, Young O. Kim, Don Kuwaye, John Motheral, Eric Saul, Robert Sasaki, Orville C. Shirey, Marshall Sumida, and Ben Tamashiro.

Fran Taylor executed the cartographic work on the endpapers and maps. Gabriel Ella and Charli Ornett did the general graphic preparation and Lorrie Inagaki handled the typing and editing of illegible manuscripts.

We are also grateful for the many additional photographs obtained through the good offices of the U.S.

_____
* Deceased

Army Signal Corps, *Honolulu Star Bulletin, Washington Post,* and *United Press International.*

Last, but not least, we wish to acknowledge our indebtedness to the many Army combat units with whom we were privileged to serve. This pictorial history is the story of World War II as seen from the viewpoint of our small pond, but we are proud to have been attached or assigned to the larger "ponds" of almost 20 different brigades, divisions, corps, armies, and army groups.

We will never forget our brave and gallant comrades of the fighting divisions of the 3d, the 34th, the 36th, the 45th, the 88th, and many others. We bask in the grand aura of their military achievements and we treasure beyond measure their fellowship and understanding.

Contents

Dedication . . . . *iii*

Author's Note . . . . *v*

Acknowledgments . . . . *vii*

Introduction:

   Senator Daniel K. Inouye . . . . *x*

   Senator Spark Matsunaga . . . . *xi*

Go For Broke *1*

Where It All Began *3*

The Birth of the 100th Infantry Battalion *13*

The Birth of the 442d Regimental Combat Team *17*

The 100th in Italy: Salerno to Foggia *26*

Action at Volturno River *35*

Attack on Cassino *39*

Next Stop: Anzio *44*

The 442d Prepares for Combat *48*

The 100th Joins the 442d *51*

The 100/442 Makes a Social Call in Belvedere *52*

The Anti-Tank Co. and the Southern France Campaign . . *64*

Crossing the Arno River *68*

Winning the Rome-Arno Campaign *73*

Rhineland Campaign — Vosges *74*

Attack on Bruyeres *75*

Biffontaine *88*

The "Lost Battalion" *90*

The "Champagne Campaign" *106*

Meanwhile, Back at the Queen's Bar in Nice *110*

The 522d Field Artillery Moves to Central Europe *113*

The 522d Opens the Gate to Dachau *117*

The Po Valley Campaign *119*

Medal of Honor *123*

Machine Gun Battalion Kesselring *126*

On to Carrara *128*

The End of the Line *136*

Peace at Last *142*

Spit-and-Polish *150*

To the Victor Belongs? *162*

Keep Up the Fight *170*

References *172*

Tables and Maps

Map: Army Groups, Armies, Corps, Divisions, Brigades — attachment/assignment of the 100/442 . . ENDPAPERS (FRONT)

100/442 Regimental Combat Team, composition . . . . *iv*

The Distinguished Service Cross, listing . . . . *vi*

Map, Eboli to Cassino *31*

Map, Anzio to Tarquinia *44*

Map, Suvereto to Orzignano *55*

Map, "The Lost Battalion" *91*

Map, "The Champagne Campaign" *109*

Map, Pietrasanta to Carrara ("The Gothic Line") . . . *125*

Map, Florida to Aulla (Po Valley Campaign) *133*

Map, La Spezia to Milano *137*

Decorations, listing *146*

Map: Campaigns, Beachhead Landings, and Presidential Unit Citations . . . . ENDPAPERS (BACK)

Daniel K. Inouye
United States Senator

DANIEL K. INOUYE
HAWAII

PRINCE KUHIO FEDERAL BUILDING
ROOM 6104, 300 ALA MOANA BOULEVARD
HONOLULU, HAWAII 96850
(808) 546-7550

United States Senate

ROOM 105, RUSSELL SENATE BUILDING
WASHINGTON, D.C. 20510
(202) 224-3934

January 7, 1982

Dear Friends:

I appreciate this opportunity to share my thoughts on the publication of this photographic history of the accomplishments of the 100th Battalion/442nd Regimental Combat Team.

I believe the achievements of this distinguished United States military unit helped to dispel in a most dramatic and bloody manner any doubts that may have been harbored as to the patriotism of Japanese Americans. Although this demonstration of citizenship was a most costly one, it did show that Japanese Americans were second to no one in loyalty and bravery.

I am proud that my country is a land of opportunity, a land which still offers the chance of success and advancement to the poor and disadvantaged. We each have a special responsibility to continually strive to make our nation a more open and just society for all.

The fight we joined decades ago will not be over until injustice and oppression are vanquished from our society.

Aloha,

DANIEL K. INOUYE
United States Senator

DKI:mcb

SPARK M. MATSUNAGA
HAWAII

WASHINGTON OFFICE:
5121 DIRKSEN BUILDING
WASHINGTON, D.C. 20510

HONOLULU OFFICE:
3104 PRINCE KUHIO BUILDING
HONOLULU, HAWAII 96850

CHIEF DEPUTY
DEMOCRATIC WHIP

MEMBER:
COMMITTEE ON ENERGY AND
NATURAL RESOURCES

COMMITTEE ON FINANCE

COMMITTEE ON
VETERANS' AFFAIRS

United States Senate

WASHINGTON, D.C. 20510

January 7, 1982

**Spark M. Matsunaga
United States Senator**

Dear Friends:

As a veteran of the original 100th Infantry
Battalion (Separate), later the First Battalion of the
"Go for Broke" 442nd Regimental Combat Team, I wish to
express my deepest appreciation to those who produced
this book honoring the Japanese American soldier. Because
memories are short and the lesson to be learned so
valuable, I believe that the story of the 100th Battalion
and the 442nd Regimental Combat Team should be told again
and again. In the sacrifices made by the veterans of the
All-Nisei Combat Team, in their courage and loyalty, we
can find the strength and determination to continue our
endless battle against discrimination and injustice--to
make ours a greater nation in a better world.

Mahalo and aloha.

Sincerely,

Spark Matsunaga
U. S. Senator

Go For Broke

Introduction

The year was 1943. Europe was in the throes of the fourth year of war with the Third Reich of Nazi Germany, and Hitler's domination of Europe was almost complete. Austria, Belgium, Czechoslovakia, France, Hungary, North Africa and Poland were ground under the iron heel of the Nazis, and smaller or more distant countries were intimidated or eliminated. England and Russia were under siege. Italy, Germany's Axis partner, bristled and chafed under Hitler's iron collar. The juggernaut of the greatest war machine the world had ever known was crunching inexorably toward global domination.

Standing in opposition were the Allies, the countries of the free world. Under the overall leadership of Gen Dwight D. Eisenhower, the Allies in Europe formed a triple tier of military defense: the Northern Group of Armies, the Central Group of Armies and the Southern Group of Armies, the latter commanded by Gen Jacob L. Devers. It was from this southern group that arose the 100/442, the unit that would later be called the "most decorated unit in United States military history."

The 100th Infantry Battalion (separate) and the 442d Regimental Combat Team fought in seven campaigns in two countries, made two beachhead assaults — one by glider — and captured a submarine. They fought the toughest troops the Nazis could throw at them — battle-wise veterans from the Afrika Korps, SS troops, Panzer brigades, and *Soldaten* from the Hermann Goering Division. Joining the great combat divisions of the 5th and the 7th Armies, they hammered the enemy up the boot of Italy and back through the Vosges Forest in France. They earned 9,486 Purple Hearts and 680 were killed in action. They were awarded 18,143 individual decorations for bravery, including: 1 Congressional Medal of Honor; 52 Distinguished Service Crosses; 1 Distinguished Service Medal; 588 Silver Stars; 22 Legion of Merit medals; 19 Soldier's Medals; 5,200 Bronze Stars and 14 Croix de Guerre, among many other decorations.

They were called by one division, "the little men of iron." Later, they would be proclaimed "Honorary Texans" by Governor John Connolly of Texas.

Who Were They?

Who were these men who made up the "most decorated unit in United States military history"? Where did they come from? What made them fight as they did?

First and foremost, they were Americans. They were like other American GIs.

They hummed and sang snatches of "Lili Marlene" and "That Old Black Magic" when these songs came crackling through the public address system. They ate

K-rations and cursed the man who invented them. They blasted the guys in the rear echelons who grabbed all the Lucky Strikes and Camels and left them with Chelseas and Sensations to smoke. They drank warm beer and were happy to get it. They took off as fast as any GI when the MPs started sweeping the Off-Limits areas. And, of course, they bled and hurt when wounded. They were typical, run-of-the-mill American GIs.

However, there were some differences.

They liked rice. Three times a day.

They had strange sounding names (Akira Okamoto, Silver Star); almond eyes (Paul Okamura, Purple Heart); black hair (Hiroshi Yasutake, Distinguished Service Cross); and brown skin (Keiji Taki, Bronze Star).

They were short. Their average height was 5'4" and their average weight was 125 pounds, even when soaking wet in the European rain, with muddy boots, loaded M1, and three grenades.

They were a quartermaster's nightmare. They wore shirts with 13½ necks and 27" sleeves; pants with 26" waists and 25" inseams. And then there were the shoes — would you believe 2½ EEE?

These were the Japanese American (Nisei, second generation) soldiers of the 100th Infantry Battalion and the 442d Regimental Combat Team. All the members of the 100/442 were Japanese Americans except for some of the officers.

● *Shorty, just about as big as nothing at all, is, we think, the shortest guy in the Army. And therein lies the problem.*

All 4'9" of PFC Takeshi Kazumura of Hilo, Hawaii, is a peck of headaches for the Quartermaster Corps.

His feet form the groundwork of the trouble — size 2½ EEE. The regiment . . . had to give PFC Kazumura 10 days' leave to travel from France, where the 442d was stationed, to Naples, where the Quartermaster Corps had two pair of shoes specially tailored for him. And, at that, still a half size too big!

When Kazumura was wounded near Cecina, Italy, where some of the toughest fighting of this hard slugging outfit took place, he was hospitalized for six weeks. When asked how the nurses treated him, he answered, "Just like a baby."

HONOLULU STAR BULLETIN

Pearl Harbor, December 7, 1941

Where It All Began

The men of the 100/442 came from Hawaii and the mainland. Their parents (Issei, first generation) were farmers, laborers, or small storekeepers. A few, a very few, had made it into the professions or into the upper economic echelons. The Issei were prohibited by law from owning property, from interracial marriages, and from becoming citizens. They were not even second-class citizens.

Following Pearl Harbor, the Japanese Americans in Hawaii were viewed with fear and suspicion. The West Coast Issei and Nisei were not only viewed with fear and suspicion, they were evacuated, relocated, and incarcerated. Like the biblical Job, who was oppressed although he had committed no wrongs, every political, economic, social, military and racist ill was cast upon

3

the mainland Japanese Americans. And like the good and innocent Job, they asked, "Why?" They were told, "It's for your own good, your own protection." So they locked up the innocent and the bewildered and threw away the key.

In Hawaii, 3,000 miles closer to the enemy, under Martial Law following a savage bombing attack, the 160,000 Japanese Americans were not relocated, were not evacuated, were not interned. They were viewed with suspicion and distrust but their constitutional rights were respected to a greater degree than were the mainland Japanese Americans'.

In all, 110,000 persons of Japanese ancestry — 70,000 of whom were native-born United States citizens — were summarily moved from their homes, their places of business, or their employment on the mainland to ten inland concentration camps (President Harry Truman's term) scattered in desolate, wasteland areas of California and several mountain and central plains states. The accommodations were hastily and crudely constructed tar-paper barracks, unpaved muddy streets and walks, paper-thin walls, communal facilities (showers, toilet, dining), and barbed-wire fences with guard towers. This was home for an innocent people and home for many of

---

Hawaii

● *You go to school, and in practically all the public elementary schools, everybody was non-Haole (non-white). We would have an occasional principal, teacher or mainland Haole. There wasn't really much contact with white persons. So little contact in any case of any kind, yeah. Everywhere you turn, on the playgrounds, in the schools, the local young kids, the athletic teams, were predominantly Japanese Americans.*

● *It was tough, you know, although my father was a tailor, he didn't make much so I never had any kind of spending money like kids today would have, and our biggest form of entertainment, I mean amusing ourselves, would be taking, let's say, a slingshot. We'd make it out of guava trees. The reason for the guava trees is because it's a nice kind of tree that gives, very pliable. And we'd take inner tubes and make slingshots out of that and knock myna birds sitting on a high-wire fence, or shooting out street lamps, you know, whatever, and going down to the river for a swim or catching opu. Opu is a little black river fish.*

Mainland

● *We lived in ghettos. A lot of people forget. We weren't allowed — our parents weren't allowed — to own property — so most of us lived in rented houses. We just never had a day to call our own. Most of us lived in great poverty. We did the very best we could but it was so restricted.*

● *The hard part was for our parents because here they were at the peak of their earning power, in their 50's, and suddenly they lost everything . . . It's really difficult for them to ever think in terms of recovery. The rest of us were kind of young and we were a little bit more flexible. We didn't understand, but we were making the best out of a bad situation.*

We lost our radios. They were turned in to the Police Department, as instructed. We didn't have any weapons in the house so consequently we didn't have to turn that in. But some of the heavier items we sold "next to nothing" . . . our furniture, dishes, family

heirlooms, and personal possessions. We had a choice of either storing it with friends or storing it at a government warehouse. At the government warehouse, we had to pay for all the transportation, the packing, and the crating. Many of us didn't have enough money to pay for that, so we did the next best thing and stored the stuff in the basement of friends, and then they would put on the seal by the U.S. Government to stop anyone from going in there, but that was a big joke. Most of the items were looted or lost.

A lot of the business people put up signs saying, "Evacuation Sale . . . Everything Must Go." They were selling things for next to nothing . . . Their losses were tremendous — some people never went back because of this situation. A lot of people turned their property over to banks to operate for them . . . hotels, apartments, their homes. As it later turned out, they weren't properly managed. When they returned from camp, years later, their properties had to be completely renovated and improved. The costs there were out of sight. They had received $12 to $19 per month for working in the camps. They had very little money.

the volunteers of the 442d Regimental Combat Team. In 1947, the President's Committee on Civil Rights would say, "This (incarceration) is the most striking mass interference since slavery with the right to physical freedom."

These actions against the Japanese Americans took place after notification by the military intelligence and by the Federal Bureau of Investigation that all potential troublemakers had been rounded up. Not one single case of espionage or sabotage by Japanese Americans on the mainland or in the islands occurred before, during or after Pearl Harbor. Yet the entire community was interned — toddling infants to 90-year old grandmothers — on military orders based on "military necessity"! Lt Gen John L. DeWitt, commander of the Western Defense Command, was quoted as saying, "A Jap's a Jap. It makes no difference whether the Jap is a citizen or not."

My husband's interned,
And my son's a soldier.
Oh, all so hard to bear,
I lament
Encaged behind wire.

— AT AN ARIZONA DETENTION CAMP
1943

● *Hey, that (Tanforan Stables) was quite a shock because we were assigned to one of those horse stalls that had been swept out, more or less, and partitioned off. The aroma was still there and here a whole family was put into one stall. We had army-type cots with straw mattresses. Any time the neighbor whispered, you could hear them. It was a strange existence because we had lived in an individual residence house where you could make all the noise you wanted to without disturbing neighbors.*

● *Inside the camp we had our curfew and our boundaries. We couldn't walk near the fences at all. We had armed guards and barbed wire surrounding the area and at the towers they had machine guns and searchlights, and then they had barbed wires with a double fence and then they had barbed wires again . . . in a couple of instances where people had strayed too close to the wire, the guard opened up. In Topaz it happened once where an individual was shot. He was looking for rocks to make a rock garden and that sort of thing.*

7

● *I had been born in the United States, raised in the United States and I have no feelings about Japan. It was kind of the "yes-yes" — "no-no" type of thing . . . the unqualified allegiance versus would you attest unqualified allegiance to the United States by saying "yes" to, I think it was, questions 27 and 28 as I recall. It was either yes, yes or no, no. Several people had indicated that — they said, no, no. Why should I sign my life away under duress, and here they have incarcerated me and suddenly ask me to volunteer and lay down my life for a country that actually betrayed me. There was this attitude and then there was the other attitude which my brother and I had right from the beginning . . . We have faith in the United States. Yes, the United States did make a mistake but we felt it was our country — right and wrong. There was never any question for us, and so our parents had asked us, whatever your decisions are, it's ours. We will not decide for you. My dad said he loves the United States . . . he lived here most of his life. He came here as a young man at 18 and he felt that this was his country and my mother felt very much the same way. One thing she did stipulate is that I don't ever forget this incident. And I said, "Oh, Mother, I could never forget this." I said, "I still have faith in the United States and this is the way I feel."*

The night of December 7th, they assembled 1,500 of us — all recruits, two weeks in the Army, drafted November 13 — took us all down to the warehouse area to load sandbags and barbed wire on trucks to take down to the beach area. We worked all day until about 10 or 11 o'clock at night. Then they said they were going to take us to an area where we were going to sleep. They took us straight down to the stockade . . . the Schofield stockade. I asked my sergeant, "Hey, how come they are putting us in the stockade?"

And he said, "Oh, according to the higher-ups, this building is the safest building around this area because it is made of concrete."

And I told the sergeant, "Don't give me that. I feel like a prisoner."

The army brass at that point did not have complete confidence in us.

My two brothers were working for the Army at one of the big airports at Kaneohe. When I got there on a pass, they told me how the marine guard poked at their lunch with his bayonet, how he bugged them so much that they couldn't eat. And here I came home on a pass from guarding the shorelines just a half a mile away. But my brothers were not the only ones bugged. When I came home, my room was ransacked. I asked my dad what happened. He said, "A couple of marines came and they turned your room upside down." I said, "For what?" He said, "Somebody told them that you were a spy or something."

One of the major factors in the development of adverse public sentiment against Americans of Japanese ancestry on the West Coast in the weeks following the Japanese attack on Pearl Harbor were the wild rumors of wholesale sabotage and disloyal conduct by persons of Japanese extraction in the Territory of Hawaii. As the campaign of hate mounted in the days before the issuance of the evacuation order, West Coast audiences were told that Japanese Americans had engaged in Fifth Column espionage and sabotage activity, had destroyed blood plasma, had blocked vital roads and had even damaged planes at Hickam Field. Some of these stories were even circulated by the chairman of a congressional committee which was investigating the necessity for wholesale evacuation. None of them, not one of the rumors, was true.
PACIFIC CITIZEN

This distrust and suspicion followed the Nisei even into their training at Camp McCoy, Wisconsin, and at Camp Shelby, Hattiesburg, Mississippi. All during stateside training a constant flow of secret, periodic reports on the Japanese American unit wended its way to the War Department. In addition, cameras, generally taboo, were issued to a favored few who took pictures of the scenery and the senoritas and any suspicious or *abunai* (dangerous) *kibei* (Nisei educated in Japan). As mentioned before, there was no espionage, no sabotage, ever, by any Japanese American. Suspicious? Only to the Caucasian eye. *Abunai?* Not one case.

Out of this atmosphere of fear and hatred, the Nisei from Hawaii and the mainland stepped forward as volunteers for an army that distrusted them. They were volunteers who had two battles to fight — one against the enemy in Europe and in the Pacific, and one against the enemy of racial prejudice in their own country. They emerged triumphant from both battles and wrote a blazing chapter of loyalty and devotion in the pages of American military history.

The following chapter begins with the story of the Hawaiian Provisional Battalion that later became the 100th Infantry Battalion.

Hawaiian Volunteers

Within two months of the bombing of Pearl Harbor, Delos C. Emmons, Commanding General of the Army in Hawaii, discharged all Japanese Americans from the Hawaiian Territorial Guard. The Nisei soldiers in the 298th and 299th regiments of the National Guard of Hawaii were also scheduled for discharge as soon as replacements from the mainland arrived.

At this critical period, several events occurred that changed this decision. The powerful and respected Honolulu Civic Association spoke out for the Japanese Americans and asked Gen Emmons to keep them in military service. The Emergency Service Committee, Morale Section, Military Governor's Office (Hung Wai Ching, Charles Loomis, and Shigeo Yoshida) also recommended that the Japanese Americans be retained in the service.

There was also the exemplary behavior of the Varsity Victory Volunteers. These discharged veterans of the Hawaiian Territorial Guard were dismayed by the Army's lack of confidence in them but their unswerving devotion to the United States led them to offer their services in whatever capacity the Army might choose to use

Above, Varsity Victory Volunteers back the War Bond drive. Left, the Army called for 1,500 volunteers, 10,000 men stepped forward

• *Near the end of December or early January, the word came down from Washington to throw all Americans of Japanese ancestry out of the Territorial Guard. Most of the* **haole** *(Caucasian) and one or two of the Chinese American officers told us they were sorry that these orders were issued. The first thing that happened was that weapons were taken away from us. In my battalion they stripped the ranks of all the noncoms. We were given honorable discharges from the HTG.*

them. They cleaned up, they cleared the ground, and they built new military installations. They did everything the Army asked and they did it with diligence and dedication.

As a result of these events, Gen Emmons reversed his decision. He recommended to the War Department that a special unit be formed to accommodate the Japanese American soldier in Hawaii. He further recommended that this unit be sent to the mainland for training and safekeeping because, in the event of another enemy attack, the Nisei might be mistaken for the enemy. Also, there was still the lingering question of their ultimate loyalty. The island GI was later to refer mockingly to this suspicious attitude as, "Who you shoot?"

On May 26, 1942, Gen George C. Marshall issued orders establishing the Hawaiian Provisional Battalion — an all-Nisei unit. Nisei soldiers were transferred from the 298th and 299th regiments to the Provisional Battalion. On June 5, the Hawaiian Provisional Battalion of 1300 men and 29 officers, under the command of Lt Col Farrant L. Turner, sailed for the mainland and combat training.

● *Yeah, we didn't have the internment to motivate us or to disapprove, but all of us were brought up in that, you know, with a family background which taught us family unity and also, in Hawaii, because we knew each other, many of us were related to each other, there was a bond that was stronger than most other military units. And if you didn't perform your part, you were letting down your neighbor, kind of a feeling that we had, so that you found very, very few cases if at all of people not performing, not performing their functions, their duty. Every guy, no matter how scary, how dangerous, felt that if a guy, if my next door neighbor is going, I'm going too. I'm going to do my job. So that to this extent I think our unit was unique in the military organization.*

Members of the Hawaiian Territorial Guard were discharged within two months of Pearl Harbor. Nisei in the Hawaiian National Guard, 298th and 299th Regiment, were not discharged. Training and duties, with some exceptions, continued as before

12

Volunteers for the Hawaiian Provisional Battalion, March 1942

The Birth of the 100th Infantry Battalion

On June 10, 1942, the Hawaiian Provisional Battalion landed in Oakland, California. Two days later, they were activated as the 100th Infantry Battalion. The "One Puka Puka" was born.

Following their activation, the 100th left by three different trains for Camp McCoy, Wisconsin. While en route, the men of the 100th had an uneasy moment — one of the trains pulled into a siding which was enclosed with barbed wire. Aware of the internment of the West Coast Japanese Americans, the islanders wondered if the same fate was in store for them. After an agonizing delay, the train slowly backed onto the main track and continued on its way.

Shortly after their arrival at Camp McCoy, the 100th Infantry Battalion was assigned to the Second Army.

The 100th trained from June to December in summer's heat and in winter's snow. For many of the Hawaiian Nisei, it was their first experience with snow. Hot or cold, wet or dry, the men of the 100th received superior ratings for their performance on the field and on the drill grounds. They also received superior marks from the townspeople for their model conduct while off the post. They earned five Soldier's Medals for heroism while not in combat for saving the lives of several local residents who almost drowned in a frozen lake.

Early Transfers

The 100th was an oversize battalion with six rifle companies (A, B, C, D, E, and F) instead of four. Shortly after their arrival at Camp McCoy, 25 EM (enlisted men) and three officers were detached and sent on a mission to Cat Island. This was a secret, special task force that conceptually and literally went to the dogs (see story in italics). The men did manage to earn yet another Soldier's Medal in addition to two Legion of Merit medals.

Another detachment of approximately 100 men was transferred to the Military Intelligence Service Language School (MISLS) at Camp Savage, Minnesota, for Japanese language training. Although hush-hush at the time, it was generally understood that these men would serve in the Pacific theater in integrated units as translators, interrogators, and interpreters.

This group was the forerunner of more than 6,000 Japanese Americans who would eventually serve in the Pacific against the Japanese enemy during World War II. The story of the heroic efforts of these men is gradually being told, but their success against the Japanese provided evidence of the Japanese American soldier's ability to fight in a nonsegregated unit against the enemy in the Pacific as well as in Europe. Many of them were decorated for valor and meritorious service against the enemy. Maj Gen Charles Willoughby, G-2, intelligence chief of Gen MacArthur's command, noted that the Japanese Americans in the MIS saved countless Allied lives and shortened the war in the Pacific by two years.

● *On November 3, 1942, Maj Jim Lovell, Lt "Rocko" Marzano, and Lt Ernest Tanaka, with 24 members of the 3d Platoon, Company B, plus Herbert Ishii, HQ Co., left Camp McCoy by airplane on an assignment of strictest secrecy. Three hours by air to the mouth of the Mississippi River, a short ride by truck from airport to pier, then an overnight journey by boat to an island.*

The men had landed at old Fort Massachusetts on Ship Island. It was ten miles long and two miles wide. The men settled into an old barracks-type building next to the Fort. This was to be their home for the next three months. Their assignment? "DOGS!" They were to help train dogs to become scout dogs, messenger dogs, "trailer" dogs, sentry dogs, suicide dogs, and attack dogs.

Daily, the men left by boat from Ship Island to Cat Island where the dogs were kept. Why a Japanese American contingent of soldiers to aid in the training of dogs? Some rear-echelon commando decided that the Japanese soldier smelled differently and that the Japanese American soldiers must give off a similar smell. It was a great idea, but it didn't work. Somebody forgot to tell the dogs. According to the Sargento of the Palmettos, Yasuo Takata, "Most of us were transferred to Cat Island to pollute the island where the dogs were with the smell of 'Jap' blood. Later results showed that this did not make any difference . . . Each dog trainer sent his dog out to find us. When the dog spotted us, the trainer would fire a shot and we would drop dead with a piece of meat . . . in front of our necks. The dog would eat the meat and lick our faces. We didn't smell Japanese. We were Americans. Even a dog knew that!"

● *The Japanese-Americans in the Military Intelligence Service (MIS) fought an entirely different kind of war than we did. They did fight the same enemy, a fanatic, militaristic enemy. They were Japanese over there, Germans over here. We were both fighting against fanatics. The Japanese-American MIS fought in Alaska, the Pacific, in China, Burma, and India. They fought with Merrill's Marauders and with General Stilwell and MacArthur. There were some 6,000 or more Japanese-Americans in the MIS as I understand it. There were some 18,000 with the 100/442 in Europe. So over all there were quite a number of Japanese Americans fighting on both fronts.*

• We had a very anxious moment there because the train pulled into the siding. It was a compound with barbed wires all around. The word quickly got around that this was a prisoner of war camp, and it looked like a prisoner of war camp, the first one we had ever seen, of course. There were guards at the corners and all that kind of thing, but then the train backed off and we continued on our way.

Right, first snow at Camp McCoy, Wisconsin, and the 100th counters it with first snow man. Below, Cat Island dog trainers take time out to do some serious fishing. Front row, Nosaka, Takata, Iwashita; back row, Ishii, Takashige.

• I remember looking out of the train window and looking back at the Rocky Mountains, you know, way off, receding away. Here were the Rocky Mountains, its formation sticking out over the horizon, and they were very, very blue mountains, you know. Then the words of "America" came to me. "Oh beautiful for spacious skies," that kind. This is what that range out there represented to me at that particular moment. It was a marvelous thing, you know, and I've never forgotten that image — seeing the Rocky Mountains off in the distance, reminding me of America.

• I know that at McCoy and at Shelby, we were probably monitored as often as any unit that ever was. We were harassed by every level from the local Army, the division, the War Department. The inspectors were stumbling over each other trying to determine whether it was possible to make a good combat outfit out of Japanese Americans. The security was far more subtle. I think we had an occasional white officer who was probably sent by Intelligence rather than to be an officer for the outfit. I'm sure that some of the observers that came from the division levels and mingled with us were probably intelligence officers. These people probably had to make reports.

15

Combat Training

In February 1943, the 100th Infantry Battalion was transferred from Camp McCoy to Camp Shelby, Mississippi for advanced-unit training. They were attached to the 69th Division. By April, the 100th was fully engaged in the Louisiana maneuvers, the graduate "war-games" course to test the combat readiness of all the participating units. These "red forces against the blue forces" war games were conducted in swamps, in mud, and torrential rain. The 100th scored tops for their performance in the field. After a two-week rest period at Camp Clai-

borne, Louisiana, the men finally returned to Camp Shelby in June.

The excellent training record of the 100th Infantry Battalion played a critical part in the decision to open the draft to all Japanese Americans. It provided support for the growing number of recommendations from respected community leaders and government officials who urged that the draft be reinstated for all Japanese Americans and that they be allowed, as American citizens, to fight for their country.

Nine months after the 100th's activation, the steady stream of petitions and interventions by prominent Americans, both civilian and military, prompted President Franklin D. Roosevelt and the War Department to re-open military service for Japanese American volunteers.

Volunteers for the 442d from Topaz Relocation Center (Utah)

The Birth of the 442d Combat Team

On February 1, 1943, the 442d Regimental Combat Team was activated. Except for the officers, who were mostly Caucasians, it was composed of Japanese Americans.

In May, approximately 1,500 volunteers from the mainland and about 3,000 from Hawaii assembled for training at Camp Shelby, Mississippi.

These volunteers did not fit the usual Hollywood version of fighting men. They were short of height and weight and bore little resemblance to John Wayne. The Nisei volunteers from Hawaii came from a setting that was tinged with suspicion and distrust. Many of the mainland Nisei came from concentration camps. Other Japanese Americans came from the Midwest, the East, the North, or the South, but they all came from a draft board rating of 4-C, Enemy Alien. The Japanese American citizen had been classified as an enemy alien short-

ly after Pearl Harbor. This act of denying the Nisei their U. S. citizenship status was unwarranted and unjustified and was accomplished without a trial, a hearing or a review.

● *The proposal to organize a combat team consisting of loyal American citizens of Japanese descent has my full approval . . . This is a natural and logical step toward the restitution of the Selective Service procedures which . . . were disrupted by the evacuation. No loyal citizen should be denied the democratic right to exercise the responsibilities of his citizenship, regardless of ancestry. The principle on which this country was founded and by which it has always been governed is that Americanism is a matter of the mind and the heart; Americanism is not, and never was, a matter of race or ancestry.*

FRANKLIN DELANO ROOSEVELT
PRESIDENT, UNITED STATES OF AMERICA

Commanding this regimental complement of Nisei volunteers at Camp Shelby were Col Charles W. Pence and his executive officer, Lt Col Merritt B. Booth. Serving in the various units of the regiment were Lt Col Keith K. Tatom (1st Battalion), Lt Col James M. Hanley (2d Battalion) and Lt Col Sherwood Dixon (3d Battalion). Lt Col Baya M. Harrison commanded the 522d Field Artillery Battalion; Capt Pershing Nakada, the 232d Combat Engineer Company; Capt Edwin R. Shorey, Cannon Company; and Master Sgt Jun Yamamoto, 206th U.S. Army Band. The Caucasian officers and leaders deserved a medal for just showing up and staying on.

Camp Shelby, Mississippi, in February 1943, was in a deplorable state — the wind blew through the barrack walls, the rain leaked through the roofs, the sand and dust got into food and bedding, and the mud made the roads all but impassable. During the early months, officers and cadre reported to camp from all points of the United States. As they straggled in, they underwent training and instruction during the day and worked as

Above, Col Charles W. Pence, commanding officer of the Combat Team returns a Chaplain Masao Yamada salute. Right, Regimental Adjutant, Tom Kobayashi prior to joining the unit at Camp Shelby, Mississippi. Note '03 Springfield rifle and WWI helmet

● *We all can remember the treatment accorded the Japanese Americans during the early years of the war when because of so-called 'racial affinity' they were torn away from their homes on the West Coast and sent to relocation camps in the interior part of the country. There they lived in almost concentration camp conditions. Our nation openly doubted their loyalty, integrity, and pride in the American way. If any race living in America should have lost faith in America, it should have been the Japanese Americans. But they defied that doubt, and finally, in 1943, they were at last given the opportunity to prove their Americanism and join our forces overseas. They had begged and petitioned for this for two long bitter years, and when they were at last given the opportunity, the response was overwhelming . . . these volunteers became "the most decorated unit in our military history . . ."*

CONGRESSMAN K. W. (BILL) STINSON

● *After Pearl Harbor, the Japanese Americans in the Army on the mainland were "collected" into groups at various posts around the country and assigned menial tasks.*

One day at Fort Leavenworth, Kansas, we were given instructions to mow the main playgrounds which adjoined the post headquarters . . . the instructions were to "keep all the men (Japanese Americans) mowing the lawn 20 feet away from the headquarters building." They were afraid some of the men would look through the windows and possibly read classified documents on the desks.

● *Even during basic training we weren't trusted. I know, because the sergeant in charge of basic training told me (when the war was over) that once a month he had to mail-drop in Hattiesburg, Mississippi, a loyalty report on each man in training. "I'm sure," he said, "somebody was writing a report on me, too!"*

● *At Fort Riley, our job was to clean out the stables. As we started to clean out the area, we received orders to drop everything and assemble on the first floor of one of the barracks. I looked out of the window and there was a 30-caliber machine gun pointing at the building we were in. Shortly thereafter President Roosevelt's car drove by. Here we were U.S. soldiers, in uniform, citizens, but they still didn't trust us.*

● *I was excited and felt we were going to the Pacific Theater at that time. I talked to a number of officers and enlisted men of Japanese American ancestry about the possibility of going to the Far East. No one had any objections. We were ready to go.*

Unfamiliar sight, infantry riding. Left to right, rear; Pvt H. Watanabe, Pvt Tadashi Kato; front, Pvt James Takahashi and Pvt James Ito. All are from Hawaii. Camp Shelby, 1943. Top, four of the five Masaoka brothers: Ben, Mike, Tad, and Ike who served with the 100/442. Henry served with the 101st Airborne. Above, a favorite southern refreshment — Hattiesburg watermelon. Left, PFC Tom Kawaguchi, the Regimental Bugler lets go with a beauty carpenters and plumbers at night. By mid-April when the first of the 4,500 volunteers began arriving, the camp was ready. The zeal and gung-ho effort of the Japanese American cadre gave some assurance to the valiant officers that perhaps the potential was at hand to weld a fighting unit.

The original 442d patch was designed by the War Department and depicted a yellow arm brandishing a red sword. The general reaction to the patch, from the Commanding Officer, Col Pence, down to the privates, was "Ugh!" Thanks to the efforts of T/Sgt Mitch Miyamoto, the 442d came up with its own handsome patch design. It showed a silver arm and hand holding a torch against a field of blue surrounded by a border of silver and red. It was a positive symbol of freedom and liberty and it was proudly worn by over 18,000 Japanese American soldiers.

Top, 232d Combat Engineers on furlough to Rohwer Relocation Center, 1943. Left, Army recruiting officer seeking volunteers for the Combat Team. Above, Mitch Miyamoto, designer of the 100/442 "liberty torch" patch, served as S-2 sergeant, 3d Battalion, when the unit went into action

The 442d started training on May 10, 1943. This consisted of the fundamentals such as military courtesy and discipline; close-order drill; the manual of arms; nomenclature, care and cleaning of equipment and weapons; familiarization with gas and grenades; day and night patrolling; covering fire; map reading; and so forth.

Nearby, the 522d Field Artillery Battalion learned how to service a 105mm howitzer, how to fire it, and how to clean it. They learned the fundamentals of setting fuse, trajectory, forward and aerial observation, and range.

At the same time, the 232d Combat Engineers took basic training and went on to learn the skills of their craft, i.e., how to build and blow up bridges, how to build and mine roads, how to cut and fill with their bulldozers and other equipment, and how to sweep mines.

"Keep smiling, our husbands are in the Army while our children grow up behind barbed wire fences." Below, the 206th U.S. Army Band, conducted by Master Sgt Jun Yamamoto. When not "on stage," the members of the band served as litter bearers and worked the supply trains

21

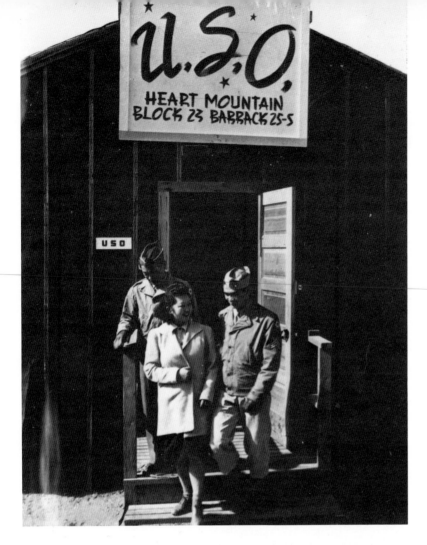

● *The relocation and incarceration of Japanese Americans caused more than property or monetary losses. In many instances, it made enemies of friends and strained relations with families. And, it all came, from the "pressure cooker" situation that the detention camps were and within which we were locked.*

In response to the pressure, some of us entered the army, some of us fought in courts, and some of us stayed in camp, sometimes defiant, sometimes compliant. The decision to go in different ways was a demonstration of our democratic upbringing. Whatever decision that was made, it was the right one. As Americans, we were exercising the right to make up our own minds. But then the "pressure cooker" syndrome took over. We began attacking one another for reaching different decisions.

Here we were, a people trapped and confined, each seeking a way out yet in our frustration striking out at our friends and family. An understandable failing then but for it to persist to this day, a tragedy.

It would seem that the ingredients of the pot have less to answer for than those who put them there.

Left and below; GIs on furlough to Heart Mountain Relocation Center, Wyoming, visit the U.S.O. Club — behind the barbed wire, of course. Right; raft, swung on cables, is pulled by men in the water! Left to right, on the raft, Pvt Charles Ouija, Pvt Francis Hirota, Sgt Harry Yamane, Pvt Fusao Hamada, and Pvt George Sunakoda

● *I was in uniform and went to visit friends in a relocation center. We checked in at the barbed-wire gate when — wham — this guy pulls out his bayonet and mounts it on his gun and says, "Okay Corporal, march." When he said, "Corporal, march," with the bayonet right behind my back, I was walking into the relocation camp. I took five steps, I turned around and said, "Corporal, take that bayonet off and put 'um back in your scabbage." He said, "No, I have to follow you with this bayonet right in back of you." So I said, "You know I am in American uniform." He said, "Yes, I know that, but these are my orders." So I took a swing at him. Then Miyamoto and the other guy held me back.*

Meeting of the 100th and 442d at Camp Shelby

By June 1943, the 100th Infantry Battalion had finished their combat readiness training in Louisiana. They then returned to Camp Shelby and found the 442d Regimental Combat Team waiting to greet them. It was a time for reunions, beer busts, and getting-together-on-passes. Brothers, cousins, and old buddies from the islands grabbed precious minutes together whenever they could.

It was also a time for some sibling rivalry. The island Japanese Americans were known as "buddhaheads" — a euphemistic rendition of the pidgin Japanese term, "buta-head," meaning pighead. The Nisei mainlanders were called "kotonks" — a term connoting the sound of an empty coconut hitting the ground. Cultural differences and missed promotions seemed to play a part in the friction between the two groups. It reached the point where several bust-ups occurred. Some overbearing and officious mainland noncoms got to be too much for the buddhaheads and the sound of empty coconuts hitting the ground reverberated at Camp Shelby. The rivalry died down as soon as the 100th was alerted for overseas duty.

In July 1943, the 100th Infantry Battalion received its colors emblazoned with the motto, "Remember Pearl Harbor." The 100th had passed its final combat test. It was now officially rated as being "combat ready." In August, the 100th Battalion left Camp Shelby for North Africa. It was to be nine long months of battle for the 100th before the 442d Combat Team would join up with them in Italy.

● *I think we all felt that we had an obligation to do the best we could and make a good record. So that when we came back we can come back with our heads high and say, "Look, we did as much as anybody else for this country and we proved our loyalty; and now we would like to take our place in the community just like anybody else and not as a segregated group of people." And I think it worked.*

The 100th Joins the 34th Red Bull Division

On August 11, 1943, the 100th was shipped out of Camp Shelby to Camp Kilmer, New Jersey. Two new company commanders were appointed: Taro Suzuki for B (Baker) Company and Jack Mizuha for D (Dog) Company. By the 20th, the 100th was in Brooklyn. The next day they were headed east on the high seas in a banana boat, the *James Parker*. On September 2, they landed at Oran, North Africa and bivouacked at Fleurus — a few miles farther inland. The Fifth Army had slated the 100th as supply train guards in North Africa. Col Farrant L. Turner would have none of it. Col Turner insisted that the 100th be committed to combat. Subsequently, the 100th was attached to the 34th Red Bull Division composed of men from Iowa, Minnesota, Nebraska and the Dakotas. The Red Bull was the first division from the United States to enter combat, and its men had fought with great distinction in North Africa. It had fought with the British to hammer the Nazis at Kasserine Pass,

Final maneuvers — next stop: combat!

North Africa, 1943, Capt Victor J. Bonin, Massachusetts, joins PFC Morio Kidani and Yasuo Takenouchi, Hawaii for chow

Americans All

The Japanese Americans fought first as Americans against the common enemy and second to demonstrate their loyalty. This is a note about a Korean American who fought double discrimination, as well as the common enemy. His military record stands as both a victorious summation and as a saga in Americanism.

• • •

When 2d Lt Young Oak Kim reported to Col Turner, the colonel's first words were, "I'll arrange for your transfer immediately."

"I just arrived," Lt Kim responded.

"Well, you're Korean; you probably don't know, but we're a Japanese American outfit."

"I know that."

"Well, you know the Koreans and Japanese [the Koreans are discriminated against in Japan] don't get along too well . . . and probably you don't want to stay here."

"No, that isn't the case at all. I don't want to be transferred," said Lt Kim. "I am an American and all the soldiers are American. We are all fighting for the same cause."

"Well, in that case you can stay. But on probation. If you get on with the men, you can stay."

2d Lt Young Oak Kim stayed. He became captain of E Company, then Executive Officer of the 100th Infantry Battalion Capt Kim earned the Distinguished Service Cross, the Silver Star, the Purple Heart with three Oak Leaf Clusters (w3olc), the Presidential Unit Citation (w2olc), and the Combat Infantryman Badge.

at Hill 609 (army term for 609 meters height), and in and around Tunis. This division had more battle experience than any other American troops at the time. The Commanding General of the 34th Division, Maj Gen Charles W. Ryder, was elated to hear that a separate infantry battalion was available. He cared little about the color or race of the troops. He needed a fighting, dependable infantry battalion. He got the 100th. The 100th took the place of the top-rated 2d Battalion, 133d Infantry Regiment, which had been designated as General Dwight D. Eisenhower's headquarters "palace" guards.

Gen Ryder planned to use the 100th in combat from the moment the unit was attached to the 34th Division. He personally spent hours briefing and giving the battalion combat orientation; he revamped the 100th's training program to better prepare them for the fighting to come.

On September 19, 1943, the 34th Division, including the 100th, left Oran and headed for Italy.

• *Once we got overseas, that feeling of being watched by the Army didn't exist. It really didn't exist. In the staging area, we were briefed by S-2 intelligence and told about different weapons and armaments of the enemy. We were briefed about wartime rules and regulations. You know the U.S. Army. We were given a brief but thorough education program. It was quite an orientation concerning the enemy and his weapons. There were no feelings of being guarded, watched or under surveillance. Combat changed a lot of things.*

The 100th in Italy: Salerno to Foggia

Company B, 100th Infantry Battalion, on the move, Italy, 1943

● *Eisenhower's staff declined them (100th) . . . Clark (took) them . . . They were superb! They took terrific casualties. They showed rare courage and tremendous fighting spirit . . . everybody wanted them . . . in the operations, and we used them quite dramatically in the great advance in Italy which led up to the termination of the fighting there.*

GEN GEORGE C. MARSHALL

● *He (Gen Charles Ryder, 34th Division) said nobody could fight in combat carrying a full field pack. He said that if you run and try to carry something like that in combat you would be so exhausted the Germans would just be able to come over and shoot you in the head as you lay exhausted on the ground. He said, "That's stupid." He said, "The most you will ever carry is one day's ration at the most. You are going to carry a poncho in the summertime and maybe in the winter time you might carry a coat, but even then I doubt that," he says. "You will carry a jacket. You will carry your food, a poncho, you will carry some socks and underwear. The socks you will pin under your arms because that is the only place that doesn't get wet and will always be dry. You will carry your ammunition and your weapons." He says, "That will be about all you can manage and even that may be too much to be able to run and fight and crawl in combat, and that is what you are going to have to do. And he said, "I don't want anybody going on 30-mile hikes anymore . . . it breaks the body down . . . I want you to take fast, short hikes. I want you to be able to hike four or five miles in an hour, alternating running and walking and marching."*

● *General Marshall . . . gave me very strict personal instructions . . . to report to him immediately the outcome in your first baptism of fire . . . after your first engagement, I said, "They . . . performed magnificently on the field of battle. I've never had such fine soldiers. Send me all you got."*

GEN MARK W. CLARK

● *We were one well-trained unit. We knew exactly what these guys are gonna do. We knew they not gonna bug out on you, they gonna protect you. So that's why we don't have any outstanding heroes. We never leave a guy out there by himself. We'll be all together. We fought as a unit. We would never leave a guy out there flat by himself and come back. We would fight together till we get everybody out or take our objective. As simple as that. A lot of times if you have an organization where you leave a guy out there by himself, the rest of the guys pull away, you gonna have a problem. You have trouble later on. But we never did that. We always stayed together and fought as a team.*

● *As far as food was concerned, they wanted a great deal more rice than was provided in the normal GI diet . . . When we were overseas, the supply and mess sergeants did everything they could, going to other units to exchange potatoes for rice. I remember one general coming up to the unit and asking, "Are you getting enough rice?" — which wasn't the first time that a general had asked that question. Every general who visited us was interested in whether or not the men were getting a sufficient quantity of rice. On this particular occasion, I turned to the general and said, "General, there's some of us Haole officers here who don't like rice."*

Above, a brief respite during training in Italy — "This is how she did that dance step in the Kansas City Steak House in Hattiesburg, Mississippi"

Right, chow line in Italy. Mess kits indicate they have yet to go into combat. Once you hit the front line, you get rid of your mess kit. It weighs too much, it's bulky, and it makes noise on patrol. The only things you carry into action are the little GI can opener, the tablespoon, canteen cup, and canteen

After a beachhead landing at Salerno on September 26th, the 100th left for their first objective: Montemarano. Their route went through the towns of Montecorvino, Eboli, and Contoursi; then north of Teora, to Lioni, and on to the San Angelo-Montemarano road. It rained the first night and it continued to rain. The 34th and the 100th were to slosh through interminable rains until the weather turned to snow and sleet, and winter set in.

The men of the 100th reached Montemarano on the 27th. The next day, the first 100th casualty occurred. 1st Lt Conrad Tsukayama, then sergeant and squad leader in D (Dog) Company, was hit by a fragment from a land mine set off by a passing jeep. He was slightly wounded in the face.

On the 29th, the 100th led the advance of the 133d Regiment on a drive to Montemilleto. Their first encounter with the enemy was at Chiusana before Montemilleto. Baker Company was on point with the 3d platoon, headed by Lt Paul Froming, leading. Time: 0915. As they moved into a clearing near a bend in the road, the Germans opened fire with machine guns, mortar, and artillery. Sgt Shigeo "Joe" Takata moved out in front. He spotted a machine gun nest and advanced while firing his Tommy gun. Sgt Takata was hit in the head by a ricochetting machine gun bullet. As he lay dying,

• *I had a platoon sergeant who carried a great big pack on his back. This pack contained mostly foodstuffs. When we got into an area where we could pull out our store, he'd cook hot rice and call me over to enjoy rice with him. If we happened to walk by a live chicken, he'd catch the chicken and cook it. I'd be invited to share the chicken. These are very important things that then seemed quite ordinary. In combat itself, these guys were just outstanding because it's a feeling of not letting down your friends, that we were in this together and we were going to get out together.*

• *All the walkie talkie operators on the line were "Buddhaheads" (Hawaiians). They would rattle off in pidgin English and the Germans could never understand them.*

One time my Tommy gun bolt stopped working right. I needed a replacement in a hurry. The walkie talkie guy relays the message, "Hama hama Tommy gun boltsu, hayaku eh?" And we needed ammo, "and ammo mote kite kudasai." Translation: "Rush order on a Tommy gun bolt and please bring up some more ammo."

• *I guess one of the things that the mainland Japanese lacked was a spirit or feeling of being together . . . they didn't have this closeness with each other that we had, coming from Hawaii. You know, we had guys that we went to school with since little kids, and we knew in the community, we knew in high school, so that there was a comradeship that started way back when, and it didn't start just in the Army.*

• *They usually let the point (first scout and second scout) go through because they know you are only the tip. The scouts travel about 25 yards apart and stay about 200 to 500 feet in front of the company. You go in front of the entire company when you hit the line. The enemy would usually let you through. They knew that one or two guys weren't that important. They wanted to know what else is behind these two jokers coming up on top. So they usually let you go through but you were always in danger because you might trip a booby trap wire or step on a mine.*

29

Lt John Ko, Hawaii — find the enemy before he finds you, Italy, 1943

What Were the First Days in Combat Like?

During the first two days of combat, the 100th had gained a hero and had made an unwilling running start on the "Purple Heart Battalion" legend. They lost 2 men KIA and 7 WIA. The Nisei were exhausted, wet and muddy. They had learned that the enemy was both methodical and lethal — the Germans zeroed-in with their artillery and mortars as they retreated; they booby-trapped trees, doorways, and dead bodies. They were tough and smart and were clever in their use of weapons and terrain. At the same time, the enemy also learned a lesson. After two days of combat with the 100th Infantry Battalion, the Germans were forced to give up seven miles of real estate, one bridge, two towns, and several road junctions. The Japanese American soldiers, like the battle-tough 34th Division, had come to fight.

Sgt Takata pointed out the machine gun emplacement to his platoon and they finally silenced the gun. Later, in a separate action, Pvt Tanaka of the 2d platoon was also killed and he became the second KIA (killed in action).

At noon the next day, elements of the 100th Infantry Battalion reached a blown bridge south of Chiusano. During the brief halt, the enemy showered them with artillery fire. Luckily, there were no casualties and the 100th moved on.

That afternoon, orders were received to move two miles across country, bypassing Chiusano. The goal was to set up a block at the road junction to the northwest. By nightfall this mission was accomplished in spite of more artillery and additional casualties.

New orders. A (Able) Company was now instructed to remain on guard at the Chiusano junction and the other elements were ordered to move on to Montefalcione — the direction from which the artillery fire was coming. It was pitch dark, but the 100th negotiated the road and the backyards of Montefalcione, and by midnight, they had ascertained that the enemy had left the area. Thus ended the second day in combat. That night the men of the 100th slept in scattered array a mile long — from Chiusano to Montefalcione.

● *He was a terrific leader — Sakai Takahashi. He was our company (B) commander. The first company commander got hit so he replaced him. Hardly anybody mentioned much about him. But I know that he was a very good combat officer.*

● *Commanding Gen Charles Ryder of the 34th Division worried about a lot of things. He was concerned that the men of the 100th didn't get enough fish; he was concerned that we didn't get enough rice; he was concerned that we didn't get the right kind of vegetables. If the men wanted to go fishing and break all the rules of the Army, he stood there and only worried about whether they were going to catch any fish. He wasn't worried about rules and regulations being broken. Gen Ryder couldn't have shown more concern and care for the men in the field.*

Pvt Tom Nose, Hawaii, raises helmet in salute to dead foe

● *For guys up in the front line, a 24-hour period is an eternity. Any second you're going to die. People who live ordinary lives just don't realize how long a 24-hour period is in combat. There, you're lucky to get any sleep; you're lucky to get any food; and death is just around the corner every second . . . 24 hours becomes an eternity, and it's an action-filled 24 hours. Sometimes it's a very calm period. But even in the calm period, you're sitting there. You don't know where you are, you don't know where you're going, you don't know what's going to happen, and you don't know when it's going to happen. It could happen in the very next minute, it could happen in the next hour. So the tension is always there. You're crouching and hiding, waiting for all hell to break loose.*

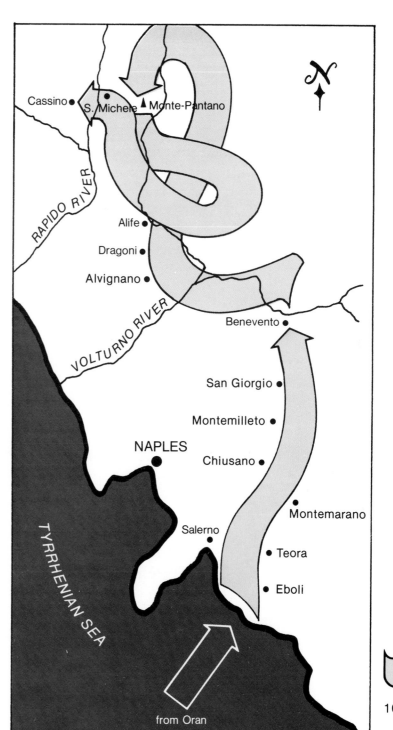

100th Battalion

The Fighting Continues

The next day, the 100th left Chiusano and pushed through Montefalcione at midnight. At dawn, the drive still continued and they reached the next town, Montemilleto, that evening. Fighting and casualties were heavy in this action. It started raining at the beginning of the drive, and the rain never let up. By October 2, the 100th had pushed through San Giorgio and Benevento and was now northwest of La Sera. They encountered artillery fire and had to dig in. The 100th held this position for two days, protecting the regiment's left flank, and were then relieved by the 45th Division.

The following excerpts from the official Army Battalion Journal entries, compiled from morning reports (sent in daily by each company on the line), provide a historical "window" on the actions of the 100th during this first week.

30 Sept 43
Co. A (point) fired upon by enemy. Eight (8) casualties incl one (1) killed. Killed: Cpl Ishii, Co. D.

To Sundry: 1,800 enemy troops at Lapio. Approximately 6,000 troops at Benevento or in general vicinity. Troops from Lapio up Lapio road.

2 Oct 43
Moved out approx 1530 to La Sera, thru S. Giorgio toward Benevento with 3d Bn on our left and 1st Bn bring up rear. Thru Benevento to secure hill southwest of city to cover advance of 3d Bn following day. Bn subjected to accurate artillery fire all night.

4 Oct 43

0430

Passwords become effective from date indicated and continue for 24 hours. 4 Oct 43. Challenge: *Washington.* Answer: *Senators.*

1650

To all Co's, 100th Bn: patrols tonight same as last night except that Co. A will furnish two motor patrols between Bn CP and 3d Bn CP in Benevento. Patrols to consist of 2 jeeps with 4 men each including driver. Patrols to cover each other during route.

1730

Boobytrap found at 680720. Trap consisted of wire attached to grapevine and other end of wire attached to an S mine which was planted in the ground. Warn all troops.

At the End of the First Week . . .

During the first week in action, from September 28 to October 4, the 100th suffered 3 KIAs, 23 WIAs and 13 injured in accidents. The cost to the enemy is best summarized by the following reports.

War Department:

". . . while acting as advance guard . . . the battalion advanced 15 miles in 24 hours, operating day and night in the face of strong enemy resistance and over difficult terrain . . . although suffering casualties, their advance continued . . . all weapons were used with complete assurance. A Japanese American sergeant who lost his life in this action has been recommended for the Distinguished Service Cross."

Gen Mark W. Clark, 5th Army:

". . . a bright spot in this period was the performance of the 100th Battalion . . . their first time in combat . . . as advance guard for a regimental combat team, they covered a distance of almost 20 miles in 24 hours, despite extreme difficulties of the mountain road. I sent a cable to Eisenhower on October 8 stating that they had seized their objectives and that they were quick to react whenever the enemy offered opposition."

Probably the most direct and most welcome reward and recognition for the 100th at this time was a terse order from the 34th Division commander, Maj Gen Charles W. Ryder:

10 Oct 43

1155

Steel helmet liners will be painted with the 34th Division insignia not later than 1800 hours 10 Oct 43. Paint is available at the Regimental Service Company.

Heading North into "Screaming Meemies"

From October 17, 1943, when the 100th left Corps reserve until November 11, the unit followed a combat line that led due north. They fought through a score of towns and villages against the Hermann Goering and other divisions and forced the Nazis to fall back through the towns of San Martino, Montesarchio, Airola, Santa Agata, Bagnoli, Limatola, and Caiazzo.

On October 18th, the 100th made their second crossing of the Volturno River. Two days later, they banged into the 29th Panzer Grenadier Regiment that was defending a road junction near San Angelo d'Alife. The enemy was entrenched behind heavily laid minefields and strongly fortified machine-gun nests. Artillery and "screaming meemies" (six-barrel rocket launchers, or, in German, *Nebelwerferen*) rained shell fragments down on the 100th. The battle raged for two days before the 100th and the 3d Battalion, 133d Regiment, drove the

Checking the Army's transport system . . .

Germans back and took over the area. It was here that Pvt Masao Awakuni single-handedly knocked out a tank with his bazooka shot and earned the Distinguished Service Cross.

Castello d'Alife was next. By 0900, 25 October, the 100th had advanced to a point approximately 1,000 yards from the crest of "Castle Hill." The fighting was bitter. They dug in. Another battalion circled and attacked the enemy from the rear in an enveloping movement. The enemy gave up the hill.

Attacked by the Luftwaffe

The 100th pressed on. In a few days, they crossed the Volturno River for the third time. The German *Luftwaffe* (Air Force) was still in action, its Messerschmitts strafing the 100th as it pushed forward. On the ground, minefields, machine guns and artillery continued to take their toll. Although the men were harassed and delayed, nothing could stop their determined drive.

Four days later, on the 29th of October, Lt Col Farrant L. Turner, who had commanded the 100th Infantry Battalion since its inception, was relieved by Maj (later Lt Col) James L. Gillespie.

On October 31, with the 100th in reserve, the 133d Regiment climbed the steep hillsides to attack and secure the heights to the north. The next day, continuing the attack, the 100th pushed through Ciorlano. The Messerschmitts came again. They strafed A (Able) and C (Charlie) Companies, wounding 12.

Action at Volturno River

Beyond Ciorlano lay the Volturno River. Here the enemy was to stage another of his deadly delaying actions.

On November 3d, the 34th Division artillery laid down a heavy midnight barrage, which the 100th followed with a crossing of the Volturno River. B Company, however, ran into thickly laid minefields. The minefields included S mines ("Bouncing Betties") that, when triggered, shot up about three feet into the air and then exploded, scattering shrapnel in a full 360-degree circle. There also were other types of mines, such as Tellers, or plate-shaped mines. These were heavy charges

used to mine roads and shoulders. They would blow up tanks, trucks and jeeps on pressure contact. There were also boobytraps. All minefields were interlocked with crisscrossing machine-gun fire. It was dark, the mines were blowing and the flares were bursting. Through these terrible obstacles, and despite heavy casualties, the men carried the fight to the enemy.

In the midst of an intense firefight, Capt Taro Suzuki of Baker Company told S/Sgt Robert Ozaki that Lt Young Oak Kim had just been wounded or captured. S/Sgt Ozaki ordered his platoon to fix bayonets. They swarmed toward a hedgerow, over a low stone wall and over a road, galvanizing the entire company into action. Lt Kim was found unharmed. In fact, he was busy throwing hand grenades at a machine-gun emplacement when he was "rescued." Whether he saved the charging men or they saved him was not important. What was important was the fact that they did not "save" the enemy. This was probably the first bayonet charge in Italy in World War II.

"Screaming Meemies" Six-barrel Nebelwerfer

● *This happened when the 100th crossed the Volturno River and had its first encounter with German troops. It was about 4:00 in the morning, and as they crossed the river, the entire front line just yelled "Banzai" and the Germans all let their guns down. They just stopped fighting. They wanted to know if the Japanese sent their people over here to fight against them. They were shocked to see Japanese Americans on the Italian front line fighting against them.*

The Battle for the Hills

On November 5, Hills 590 and 610 fell to the 100th. Enemy resistance on and around Hill 600 was especially stubborn. Continuing artillery fire and repeated counterattacks were mounted even after the hill was taken. Typifying the determination of the 100th was the bold and skillful direction of mortar fire by three forward observers — Lt Neill M. Ray, Cpl Katsushi Tanouye, and Cpl Bert K. Higashi of D Company.

On November 6, these men took up a position in advance of the rifle companies and directed mortar fire at the counterattacking enemy so effectively that the Germans withdrew. Later that day, all these men, trag-

● *I didn't go in to prove myself American because I knew I was a good American. Right through, I mean, from the beginning. Before the war I was a good American. I went in the war because I didn't like Hitler and Tojo. I didn't like their pogroms, the killing of the Polish people, and Jewish people, and they're the master race thing. I mean that was the thing that drove me. I remember the first sermon I gave in Shelby was concerned with this. I said if you came here to prove yourself a better American, that you are a good American, you might as well go home. But if you came here because you wanted to defend democracy and brotherhood and equality, then that would be a worthwhile thing to fight for. And that's what we fought for.*

ically, were killed by tree bursts from artillery. Each was awarded the Silver Star.

On November 11, 1943, the men of the 100th were relieved once again by units of the 45th Division. After a month and a half of combat, the 100th had suffered the loss of 3 officers KIA, 75 enlisted men KIA and 239 WIA or injured in action. The 100th now pulled back to rest and refit until the day before Thanksgiving.

At great cost in men and materiel, they had pushed a stubborn enemy from Salerno to Pozilli. Although replacements came in, they did not come in fast enough to keep pace with the casualties. After slightly more than a month of fighting, the 100th Infantry Battalion already was under full line strength. They were truly the Purple Heart Battalion.

Within two weeks, the 100th was again called back into action. Their mission: to lead a frontal assault on the hills near Colli-Rochetti and clear the Colli-Atina road so that the 34th Division could outflank the German defenses at Cassino.

In a heavy rain of artillery, rocket, mortar, and machine-gun fire, across fields studded with mines and boobytraps, the 100th advanced against the enemy. After several days of intense fighting, they took three key hills: 905, 920 and 1017. For nine days they held the ground, they fought, and they patrolled. But their flanks could not catch up to them. On December 9, they were relieved by the 2d Moroccan Division, French 1st Army.

The fighting in the hill area (La Croce/Monte Marrone) was so bitter that Company C had only 50 men left out of a normal complement of 187. All personnel from the extra (now defunct) rifle companies, E and F, had been pulled out and sent in as replacements for the 100th. The 100th suffered over 200 additional casualties. Its commanding officer, Lt Col James Gillespie, became ill and had two replacements within a 24-hour period: Capt Alex E. McKenzie and Maj Caspar Clough, Jr., a sea-

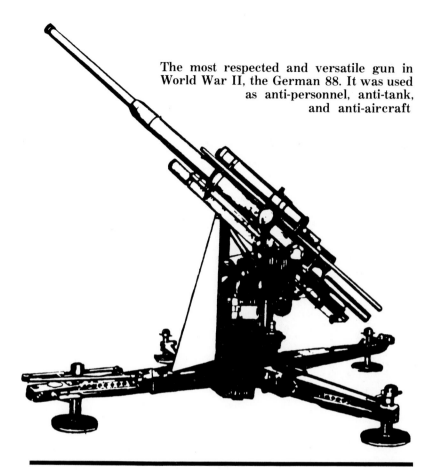

The most respected and versatile gun in World War II, the German 88. It was used as anti-personnel, anti-tank, and anti-aircraft

● *You have to have the will, you have to have the desire, and you have to have the spirit. It's a mind over matter situation. You can go without food, you can take extreme cold, you can take extreme heat, you can take anything if you make up your mind you can and you will do it, and that's really what it takes. For example, before the battle of Cassino, we were in the mountains fighting the SS forces, we were in two feet of snow, we had no winter clothing, no special boots. We were wearing the regular things that the American soldier wore on a parade field — an Eisenhower jacket and that's really no protection for snow. We went without sleep for three nights. We walked and hiked every night even though there was a blizzard every night. We fought two out of the three days we were up there.*

soned battalion commander with the 1st Division in North Africa. All jobs with the 100th were dangerous.

In early January 1944, the 100th went on a reconnaissance in the Radiosa Hills sector. A week later, they attacked in the Majo Hills mass. On January 11, they took Hill 1109. On the 13th, they took Hill 1207 and on the 14th, Hill 692. These were a series of snow-covered mountains overlooking Cassino. Most of these hills were taken during the onslaught of a fierce blizzard. On the 15th, the town of San Michele fell to the 100th. The main Gustav Line of the enemy was now encountered.

● *This story is about us being in the front lines at the foot of Cassino where we were pinned down under heavy fire. You know the way an Italian home is made — just stacks of rock and nothing, no reinforcement. The Company CP was in one of the farmhouses. We were in a bracket of mortar fire. All we could do was sit down on our steel helmets and pray. And we had mortars firing over us, short, and this man — Ohara, with his legs spread wide and was facing down, and the mortar shell came right through the roof and right between his two legs, in front of me. For about 2 or 3 seconds, we turned white as sheets, we couldn't talk, but we are home today to tell the story. It was a dud.*

Attack on Cassino

The weather was now raw and cold. The men fought not only the enemy but the mud and rain. Oh, to be back in sunny Hawaii!

On January 24, 1944, the 100th was back on the line and pressing the initial attack against Cassino. They faced the 1st German Parachute Division, a crack SS division entrenched in the Gustav Line. Again, the Germans had the advantage of terrain and made full use of it.

The first task of the 34th/100th was to cross the Rapido River. The area was swept by artillery, mortar, and machine-gun fire. All buildings and trees had been completely demolished by the Germans. The ground for over 200 yards before the Rapido River was flooded and

The mountainous terrain of the Cassino-Mignano-Esperia area. Italy, December 1944

knee-deep in mud and mines. During the first night, under a heavy cover of artillery fire, Companies A and C of the 100th moved to the river wall.

The next night, Maj Dewey, taking command of the 100th, with Maj James Johnson, Regimental Executive Officer, and Captain Mitsuyoshi Fukuda, Commander of A Company, made a further reconnaissance of the A and C Company line of attack. They were caught in a hail of artillery and machine-gun fire and dispersed into a mine-field that blew up beneath them. Major Johnson was killed and Maj Dewey was wounded. That night, Maj Clough was reinstated in command of the 100th. On the next day, in broad daylight, B Company tried to follow A and C to the river but was caught in hostile artillery and machine-gun fire. Only 14 out of their 187 made it to the wall. Seriously depleted in ranks, stripped of their top command, the battalion was ordered to San Michele for reorganization.

● *You can't say too much for the medics. They were really great. They had this buddy or team spirit of the Hawaiians to the nth degree. Whenever someone got hit, the medics would be there to take him out. The medics would run out there under fire and grab those guys. A lot of times they got hit and killed. But they never failed to help us and bring us in, small arms fire or whatever. Nothing stopped them. We have nothing but the highest praise for the medics.*

● *I'd go out — at the front believe it or not — they'd call me up on the phone. "Chaplain when are you coming to give a service." You know — at the front. And that couldn't be — I couldn't bunch them together. They'd be in their own foxholes, you know. If a shell came, it would kill a whole bunch if they gathered together. And I was scared too. I didn't stay very long, just about a scripture and a prayer. That's about all, you know. And talk with the boys a little bit and then take off.*

41

The Orders Remain: Attack!

On January 29, Maj James W. Lovell, just released from the hospital, assumed command of the battalion. His job was to ready the 100th to attack a castle halfway up the mountainside on the way to the Cassino monastery.

On February 8, in the dead of winter, the 100th attacked. Against light resistance, they moved up the barren terrain and secured Hill 165. However, the right and left flank units were unable to keep pace with the 100th. The 100th dug in deeper and held the hill for four days but fierce resistance on the flanks still made the position perilous. The 100th was then ordered back behind the hills adjacent to Cassino to join the regimental reserves.

On the first day of this action, Maj Lovell was wounded again. Major Clough, having recovered from his wounds, resumed command of the battalion. Shortly thereafter, Maj Clough was wounded again. 1st Lt Young Oak Kim now commanded the 100th. By the time the war was to end, the 100th Infantry Battalion would have 13 changes of battalion commanders. In this battalion, nearly everyone earned a Purple Heart. The lucky ones got two or three and lived to tell about it.

On February 18, the 34th Division launched its final attack on Cassino. The men stormed the defenses of Monte Cassino again and again, but the enemy was strongly entrenched and well-equipped. The ranks of the 34th were depleted, especially the 100th Battalion. They had gone in under-strength and had lost about 200 more men. One platoon had moved into line with 40 men. They came down from the hill with only five. The 100th did regain the ground halfway up to the stone Abbey, but flank support again was non-existent. After four days of intense fighting and holding, the 100th was ordered back to Alife for replacements and reissue of equipment.

The 100th had fought gallantly and bravely with the 34th. Cassino had been within their grasp, but before they could accomplish the final takeover, they ran out of men and materiel. For the 34th Division, this ended the fighting for Monte Cassino. Army records later noted that five divisions finally were required to take Cassino. The 34th Division had almost made it alone.

"... now down to one officer per company ... riflemen down to 15 or 20"

The ruins of the Mount Cassino Abbey -- it took bombers and five divisions to reduce it -- the 34th (100th) almost did it alone!

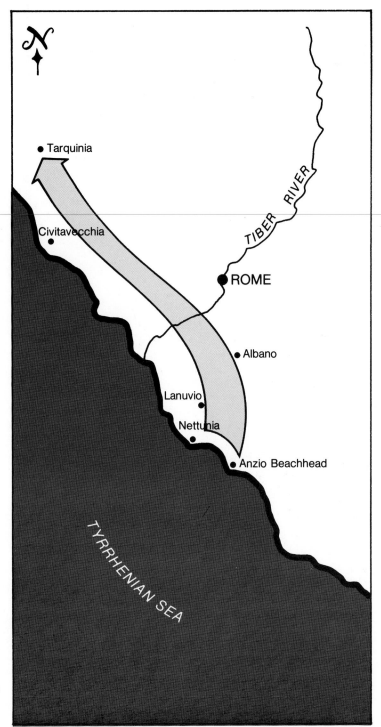

Tarquinia

Civitavecchia

TIBER RIVER

ROME

Albano

Lanuvio

Nettunia

Anzio Beachhead

TYRRHENIAN SEA

100th Battalion

Next Stop: Anzio

Reinforced with over 200 replacements, the 100th Infantry Battalion, now operating as a separate battalion directly under Gen Ryder's command, jumped out of the frying pan that was Monte Cassino into the fire that was Anzio. The date: March 26, 1944.

Anzio was an Allied beachhead about 10 miles square. The beachfront property was subjected to every type of exploding device the Germans could dump on it — aerial bombs; artillery, rocket, and mortar barrages; machine-gun and small-arms fire; flares; and let's not forget, the shells from the Anzio Express, a massive railway artillery gun. The Allies, equally determined to remain, poured in men and equipment in even larger numbers. For two months, the jockeying continued. The Germans shelled and fired on Anzio throughout the daylight hours. It was not safe to be outside while the sun was up. At night, the 100th bolstered its defenses while patrols probed the enemy strength and positions.

On May 11, the entire front exploded. The British and the French pushed forward in their respective sectors. The Americans pushed forward to break out of Anzio with Rome as the objective.

On June 2, the 34th was ordered to take the high ground of Lanuvio and La Torretto — towns where the enemy's stubborn resistance had created a bulge in the

---

• *Another fellow was hit in the back with a dud and fell to the ground. Amazingly, he reached over, grabbed the dud, and ran with it in his arms a safe distance from his buddies where he threw it away. He collapsed and fell again. It was amazing because he had a broken back.*

"When you have seen these boys blown to bits, going through shellfire that others refused to go through, sleep, when they could, in foxholes half full of water, and other horrors not to be mentioned — then is the time to voice opinion. Not before.

"This perhaps doesn't apply to all folks of Japanese descent, but you should see some of the others that call themselves Americans. If you care for any more opinions of other members of this division, ask for them.

"We who have the privilege to be beside them in combat are proud of such a fact. From some papers we have had the privilege of reading, it seems a few are glad to give these boys a small amount of credit, which belongs to such Americans. To those concerned we also hope 'our boys' may continue to prove their courage and ability to gain more valor and distinction."

The letter declared that "it made our blood boil" to read some of the letters submitted to the **Register** from Iowa readers.

The letter was signed by the following soldiers from "somewhere in Italy": S/Sgt Edward G. Schoa, Pvt Harold Zollner, Sgt Harold Knude, Sgt Harold Kerch, Cpl Robert Howell, S/Sgt George R. Vipoud, and T/5 Harold A. Allen of Kansas.

PACIFIC CITIZEN

● DES MOINES, Ia. — *Declaring "it's about time some of the folks back home are put straight on some things," six Iowa soldiers and one from Kansas have signed a joint letter to the* **Des Moines Register** *in which they declare they are proud to fight side by side with Japanese American soldiers.*

The letter in the Des Moines paper referred to letters in the **Register** *which criticized Japanese Americans in Iowa.*

"We are Iowa boys of the 34th Division, and have fought side by side with the boys of Japanese descent whose pictures appeared in your edition of Feb. 13," the soldiers wrote to the **Register.** *The soldiers' letter added:*

"We know plenty of folks that call themselves Americans that have done much less to prove they give a hang about their country.

"Whenever you have been near enough to see these boys die for their country, then is the time to voice your opinion. There have been times when these Japanese, as you call them, have saved many lives, only because they have proven themselves better Americans than some that were not of Japanese descent.

45

Top left, Company B, 100th, moving into line. Bottom left, riding through Rome...learning that the younger children had never tasted chocolate candy! Above, treasured inscription from the 34th Division Commanding General, Charles W. Ryder — a soldier's soldier. Top right, Dog Company on the move, point is Victor Yamashita, followed by Yobun Nobara and Arthur Kuwahara — all are from Hawaii. Bottom right, Nisei guard bringing in the prisoners

Allies' charging line. The 100th spearheaded the drive, and, after a two-day battle, Lanuvio and La Torretto fell. The road to Rome was open. In this action, the 100th earned six Distinguished Service Crosses and one Silver Star. Their casualties included 15 killed, 63 wounded, and 1 missing in action. Tragically, that evening, friendly artillery fire fell short on the men of the 100th, killing and wounding several before the firing could be brought under control.

During the next two days, under the command of the most recent battalion commander, Lt Col Gordon Singles, a West Point officer, a task force crushed the last elements of resistance at Genzano. Then, in rapid succession, the 100th spearheaded the attack through Arricia, Albano, and Fattochie until they were only seven miles from Rome. At this point, the 1st Armored Division geared up and moved on into Rome.

At 2200, 5 June 44, the 100th boarded trucks and rolled through Rome to an assembly area a few miles beyond its bounds. Rome had been declared an "open city" by the Germans and was thus spared destruction and ruin.

The next day, the 100th convoy stopped at the western seacoast town of Civitavecchia, 40 miles northwest of Rome. It was here at last that the 100th Infantry Battalion caught up with the 442d Regimental Combat Team. Date: 15 June 1944.

● *Chaplain Yost stayed with us all the time. He stayed at the heat of the battle and took care of the wounded. He was one of the finest men that I've ever met in my life, and the men flocked to him for several reasons. One, they were looking for something, some faith, whether it's a Christian faith or the Buddhist faith. The other thing, they admired Chaplain Yost.*

The 442d Prepares for Combat

Company E, 2d Bn, 442d Regimental Combat Team, in formation, Camp Shelby, Mississippi, June 1943

While the 100th was in nine months of bitter combat, the men in the 442d underwent final combat training at Camp Shelby, Mississippi, and sent over replacements for the 100th as needed. In the past six months, the 442d had sent 530 enlisted men and 40 officers to replenish the battered ranks of the "Purple Heart Battalion." In addition, 19 enlisted men and four officers were transferred to the Office of Strategic Services (OSS). These men underwent secret, special intelligence training at Fort Sheridan, Illinois. After training, they were sent to the China, Burma, India Theater of Operations. Some worked behind the Japanese lines gathering military intelligence for the U.S. Army.

During combat training, the men of the 442d would field-strip rifles, move double-time on marches, and hurl grenades. Then they would work together in larger and larger fighting units. It was the period for blending and meshing the operations of squads, platoons, companies, battalions, and regiments as cogs in the juggernaut of division and army. It was the full and efficient fusion of all the components of the Combat Team — the coordination of the rifle companies, battalions, and regiment with artillery, cannon, engineers, anti-tank, heavy weapons, and I and R (Intelligence and Reconnaissance). Unit training meant days and weeks in the field under simulated combat conditions. This was the make-or-break period for final stateside training before going overseas.

• *Hey lieutenant, you from the One Puka Puka?*

Yes, I'm from the 100th . . . from Kauai. What island are you from?

Oh, me not from Hawaii. Me one kotonk from Chicago.

*How come you talk like a **buddhahead** (Islander)?*

If I no talk like this, I get "bust up" (dirty licking).

SENATOR SPARK MATSUNAGA

The Mississippi Mud

From October 1943 through February 1944, with a few days off for Thanksgiving and Christmas, the men and officers of the 442d trained in the hills and swamps of Mississippi. In the process, the troops took on not only feigned enemy forces but real, live water moccasins; they also learned about large-unit tactics and support as well as how to get along with mud and chiggers. They learned a lot about nature but most important of all, they learned how to operate as a military team.

The effectiveness and determination of the men of the 442d and their fine performance in various practice skirmishes did not go unnoticed. The War Department was so impressed with the results of the final training phases of the 442d that the civilian Nisei status was reclassified from 4-C ("Enemy Alien") to 1-A (eligible for the draft). This action restored the rights and privileges of citizenship which had been summarily and unjustly denied to the Nisei since shortly after Pearl Harbor.

On March 4, 1944, the 442d Regimental Combat Team was reviewed by Army Chief of Staff, Gen George C. Marshall. After a quick, intense inspection and a few words to the men, the General left. Two days later, orders were received, "prepare for overseas movement."

The 442d Heads Overseas

In April, the 442d was sent to the staging area at Camp Patrick Henry, Virginia and by May 1, they were rocking in the queasy holds of Liberty ships off Newport News, Virginia. That evening the 442d, minus the 1st Battalion left behind as cadre for replacements, sailed from Chesapeake Bay. They were part of a convoy of over 100 ships headed east across the Atlantic. A convoy can only move as fast as its slowest vessel — in this case, the Liberty ship with a speed of about eight knots or so. The trip took 28 days which translates into approximately 2,400 poker hands or 4,600 crap games. For two weeks, nobody knew where the outfit was headed. When the little GI booklet on how to converse in Italiano was issued, the men knew it was "Bon giorno, paisano."

On June 2, 1944, the 442d debarked in the demolished harbor of Naples and bivouacked at Staging Area No. 4 near the little town of Bagnoli, ten miles inland. Equipment was uncrated, cosmolene and waterproof packings removed from weapons and gear, and land legs were substituted for sea legs. Some of the men received passes to visit the ruins of old Pompeii to see the X-rated frescoes and to purchase X-rated souvenirs.

A few days later, the men left Naples for Anzio aboard rolling LSTs and rocking LCIs. One seasick Regimental Combat Team debarked at Anzio beachhead, and wended its way on wobbly legs for five wretched miles to a bivouac area outside the port, where the men collapsed.

● *We went over right after training. We went to Newport News, where we debarked. We got on board a Liberty ship. The Liberty boats were built in a hurry — they were little boats. I think their top speed was 10 knots per hour, about 13 miles per hour. It took us 28 days to get across. We were with a huge convoy. There must have been a hundred ships, and the convoy can only go as fast as the slowest ship. I swear we were on the slowest ship. It just seemed that way, of course. There were cruisers, subchasers, submarines, everything you can name was floating alongside us — zooming in and out on the way over. It took us 28 days, it was a long time.*

I was not seasick to the point of throwing any of my meals away. But I was really nauseated.

A friend of mine, Kobe Shoji, had broken his arm just as we're about to leave. He could have stayed behind but insisted on coming over. He came over with his broken arm and all.

An enjoyable experience was coming up out of the hold of the ship at night where we were sleeping. (We slept on bunks — five high. I decided that if I got seasick I was going to get sick on top. I didn't want to be on the bottom bunk if somebody got sick, so I grabbed the top bunk.) So anyway the story I want to get to is about coming up on deck for fresh air at night because we got all this foul air down in the hold where we got hundreds of sick guys. So you go up on deck for fresh air. So what's interesting on deck at night for a landlubber? What's interesting is to look over the rail, midocean, and see fluorescent fauna and flora floating by — "lightning bugs" of the ocean, underneath the ship, going by. To watch it was just amazing. We didn't know all these plants and animals had lights and such things. During the day, huge jellyfish and whales would appear. We saw some huge "things" off in the distance. Then there were strange sounds and groans at sea. We had to assume they were large fish and friendly. But this was our trip going over. Mostly we played cards, told tales and got to know each other well. All this time, the ship was rocking and rolling. We finally hit Naples on the 28th day. We had a couple of alarms at sea about attacks, but they were all false.

That night, 7 June, German airplanes raided the ammo dumps in and around Anzio . . . it was the first time that the 442d was under fire. It looked like a Fourth-of-July spectacle, only someone could get hurt. There were arcing red-tracer streaks accentuated at sky-level by loud, punctuating flak bursts. On the ground, the dumps were catching hell. Bomb bursts flashed and clouds of smoke and dust rose in the air. The attack broke up their outdoor movie, and the 100/442 men scattered for cover. A 442d man on ground duty was struck on the helmet by shrapnel. Later, it was learned that several companies of the 2d Battalion were still aboard LCIs when the raid took place. Luckily, no one was injured.

The 100th Joins the 442d

The 442d Combat Team left Anzio on the 9th and arrived at Civitavecchia, north of Rome, on the 10th. The Germans were dug in a few miles away. The 442d was attached to the 34th "Red Bull" Division. The 100th Infantry Battalion, which had been assigned to the 34th Division, now became attached to the 442d Regimental Combat Team, taking the place of the 1st Battalion left behind in Camp Shelby.

The 100th Infantry Battalion was allowed to retain its separate designation because of its outstanding battle record. It had started out with 1,300 Japanese Americans from Hawaii. By the time they joined the 442d, they had suffered over 900 casualties. Many of the replacements for the 100th had been "mainlanders" from the 442. Now the two Japanese American fighting units were united.

For a brief period of about two weeks, brothers, cousins, and old acquaintances mingled and "shot the breeze" amidst field briefings on the enemy and final brush-up training sessions together.

On the 26th of June, the 442d, with the 100th as its new first battalion, moved into combat. The objective: Belvedere and the road to Sassetta.

100/442 Makes a Social Call in Belvedere

Suvereto -- the 442's introduction to combat

With the 2d and 3d battalions in advance and the 100th in reserve, the Combat Team moved northward to Suvereto to relieve the men of the 517th Parachute Infantry Regiment and of the 142d Infantry Regiment while en route to Belvedere. Heavy enemy artillery and tank fire forced them to stop. Grabbing a 60mm mortar and going forward alone, PFC Kyoshi Muronaga produced such accurate and intense fire that the enemy's 88mm battery withdrew. Killed in action, PFC Muronaga was awarded the Distinguished Service Cross for bravery.

However, machine-gun fire and counterattacks from hilltop positions continued to hold up the advance. Now the 100th was pulled out of reserve. In a military version of the "quarterback sneak," they attacked right up the middle, between the 2d and 3d battalions. Moving quickly and fighting efficiently, they dismantled an entire Hermann Goering combat battalion in an afternoon. Their rapid breakthrough up the center cut off all the enemy's lines of retreat and freed the 2d and 3d battalions. Then the 100th started on a house-by-house clean up of Belvedere and took this objective late that same afternoon. The 2d and 3d drove the remaining Germans off the hills and down onto the roads where the 100th was waiting for them with guns and mortars at ready. Only a few of the enemy escaped and they did so by running in complete disorder into the hills.

For the Belvedere and Sassetta actions, the 100th was to receive their first of three Presidential Unit Citations. Their toll of the enemy was 178 dead, 20 wounded and 86 captured. They destroyed 8 trucks, 19 jeeps, 13 motorcycles, 3 self-propelleds, 2 anti-tank guns, 2 tanks, 2 half-tracks, 2 command cars, and an 80mm mortar. In summary: one SS combat battalion was completely destroyed. The 100th suffered 4 men killed and 7 wounded.

The 100th's fighting momentum was sustained for four days. Spurred on by the example of the 100th, the 2d and 3d Battalions came alive and began to function as a team. The 442d Combat Team took the towns of Sassetta and Castagneto. These actions were significant not only as military victories but also as morale boosters, especially when the men liberated a fully equipped bar — cognac and vino up front and pigs and chickens out back!

Sassetta – the 100th leads the way

The Japanese-American 100th Infantry Battalion, which recently received a citation from Lt Gen Mark W. Clark, U.S. Army, commanding general of the Fifth Army, has participated in fighting on virtually every front established in the drive through Italy, reports from Fifth Army Headquarters indicate.

Going into action first in the Naples area, the battalion fought its way across the Volturno River and the Rapido River and was in the front line for 40 days at Cassino. Later it was transferred to the beachhead at Anzio and took part in the breakthrough to Rome.

The 100th Battalion and the 442d Regimental Combat Team, of which it is a part, are composed of Americans of Japanese descent, all of whom volunteered for service. The majority of the soldiers in the 100th are from the Hawaiian Islands.

The mission for which the battalion was cited was accomplished June 26 and 27 in the vicinity of Belvedere and Sassetta, Italy. A strong German center of resistance dominated a vital highway and impeded the advance of an American infantry division. In the face of numerically superior forces of Nazi infantry and field artillery, the battalion fought its way to the defended positions and completely destroyed the enemy flank position, killing 178 Germans, wounding 20, and capturing 73 in the process.

In ten months of almost continuous fighting only two soldiers of the 100th Infantry have been captured by the Germans, while the battalion has taken hundreds of prisoners, killed hundreds more and destroyed vast quantities of enemy materials.

More than 1,000 Purple Hearts, 44 Silver Stars, 31 Bronze Stars, 9 Distinguished Service Crosses and 3 Legion of Merit medals have been awarded to members of the unit. Fifteen enlisted men have received battlefield commissions after displaying outstanding leadership in combat. Among them are company commander, Capt Mitsuyoshi Fukuda, of 2333 Fern Street, Honolulu, Hawaii, and battalion commander, Lt Col Gordon Singles, of Denver, Colo., a West Point graduate.

There never has been a case of desertion or absence without leave in the 100th, although there were two reported cases of "reverse AWOL." Before their battle wounds were completely healed in a field hospital behind the lines, two soldiers left the hospital and hitch-hiked back to their companies on the battlefield.

ARMY-NAVY REGISTER
AUGUST 12, 1944

On to Luciana

After a two-day rest, the 100/442 moved back into line and on 1 July crossed the Cecina River. This was the route to Luciana and to the high ground overlooking the seaport complex of Livorno (Leghorn). Whoever controlled Luciana, controlled Livorno. The enemy would not surrender this easily.

For two weeks, the 100/442 had fought with the German army in almost continuous battle. Everything the enemy could muster was thrown at the Combat Team — artillery, mortar, machine-gun, and small-arms fire. Mines and boobytraps lay underfoot, but the Combat Team continued to trudge on in dogged determination. They seized Hill 140 ("little Cassino") and the towns of Castellina, Pastina, Pieve di San Luce, Orciano, and Lorenzano.

Luciana finally fell after two days of bitter house-

● *During our first attack on Luciana, Company K lost most of its officers, including the company commander. Lts Collins and Hayashi were the only platoon leaders left to continue the attack. Lt Hayashi took over operation of the company. Our first Command Post (CP) was a house on the edge of town which was being constantly pounded by artillery and mortar fire, so we left. The house was demolished by a direct hit. A second CP was set up in another house closer in toward town. Lt Wood, the Forward Observer (FO) for the 522d Field Artillery Battalion, spotted a German tank near a house several hundred yards in front of us. To prevent the Germans from learning about our plans, Lt Hayashi called in artillery fire directions in Japanese over the SCR 300 radio. The artillery fire demolished the house and trapped the tank in fallen debris. With the tank out of the way we were able to move along the road leading up to a church on the high ground. This was the same road where T/Sgt Atsushi Sakamoto*

of the 1st platoon was killed earlier in the day while leading a patrol. Then suddenly, from out of nowhere, PFC Oliver Hayashi yells and throws a diving tackle at Lt Hayashi. They both go down. A second later, machine-gun fire rakes the spot where they had been standing moments before. PFC Hayashi, no relation, had saved Lt Hayashi's life. But the war was still on. The lieutenant called for fire on the window where the machine-gun fire came from. It got awfully quiet after that. Later the same day, plans were made to attack the house where the fire came from. A strong enemy force was entrenched there. S/Sgt Shibata was to take a squad from the 1st platoon and make a diversionary frontal attack while the lieutenant with the rest of the company was to come in from the flank and rear. After the joint attack, we took cover behind a stone wall in the rear of the house. The fixed machine-gun jutting out of the second story window couldn't angle down and hit us. We lucked out. The Germans didn't. The lieu-

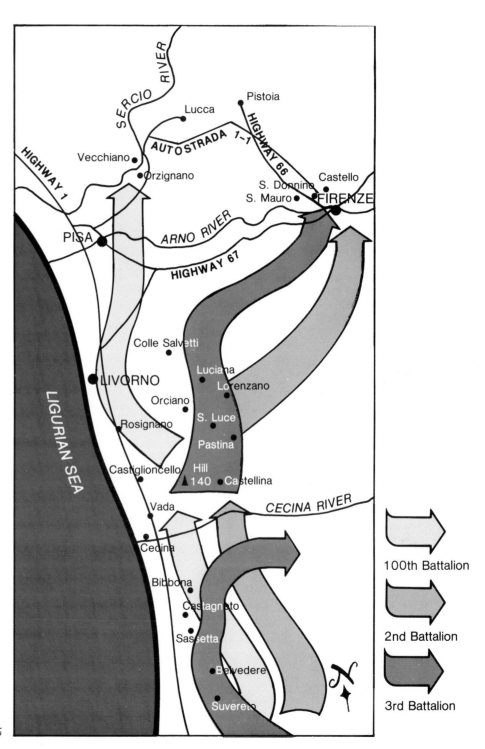

tenant called a bazooka team to the wall and started shelling the second story window. After we silenced the gun, we rushed over to the side of the house and began firing and lobbing hand grenades into the lower windows. In a short time, a white flag comes poking and waving from one of the lower windows. We hold our fire and out comes 21 Germans dressed in camouflage jackets, all from the 16th SS Panzer Grenadier Regiment. A 22nd prisoner is captured the next morning when Lt Hayashi went to check the latrine. There was a German sound asleep on the floor. He was quickly made prisoner and sent to the rear. That was our bag for two-days of fighting in Luciana: 1 liberated town, 1 tank and 22 prisoners. Later, bedlam broke loose when we found the townsfolk. The Germans had herded them all together into one of the largest cellars in town. They weren't hurt, but they were mad at the "tedeschi" (Italian for Germans) for keeping them hostage.

55

Livorno

● *"Activated on February 1, 1943, in response to request of many loyal American-born Japanese to serve in the Armed Forces, the 442d set a high standard of training at Camp Shelby, Mississippi. The Japanese Americans arrived in Italy late in May, 1944. The famous Japanese American 100th Infantry Battalion, already fighting in Italy and composed of former activated Hawaiian National Guardsmen, became the first battalion of the new regiment. The 100th Battalion was one of the first ground units to receive the Presidential Unit Citation for fighting in Italy.*

"This citation arose from the battalion's outstanding performance in the vicinity of Belvedere and Sassetta, when it was assigned to the mission of neutralizing a strongly defended German position. The men fought a numerically superior enemy, killing 178 and sending the remaining Germans reeling back in a demoralized retreat."

"The new regiment went into action late in June and distinguished itself in the bitter fighting for the approaches to Leghorn, Pisa and Florence. The toughest Wehrmacht SS units faced the Japanese Americans in their first engagement in the mountainous regions guarding the approaches to key German defenses in northern Italy."

"Before the regiment was relieved it had liberated 11 towns and villages. The men stormed and took two major hills, Hill 140, known as Little Cassino, and Hill 132. Their forward movement enabled other elements of the Fifth Army to forge ahead. At the port of Leghorn the 442d protected the entire flank of the Allied drive and permitted armored infantry units to enter the city. Japanese American patrols were the first to penetrate into the historic and strategic city of Pisa."

"During this drive the regiment killed 1,124 Germans, captured 331 and wounded several hundred, figures which do not tell the whole story because they do not include the dead buried by the enemy nor wounded evacuated by him. At the same time the regiment swept up vast quantities of enemy material—cars, motorcycles, trucks, Mark IV tanks, antitank guns, self-propelled guns, field artillery pieces, mortars, machine guns and small arms of all types. PACIFIC CITIZEN
MAY, 1945

Left, 2d Lt Masanao Otake, Hawaii, leads his platoon from Orciano toward Livorno and the enemy. Above center, moving men and mortar shells (men in rear are sitting on shells). Above right, "win some, lose some," we won these — prisoners heading for the rear. Left, liberated small business machine (tank, German)

to-house fighting by Company K of the 3d Battalion, with support from the 2d Battalion on the flank and fire support from both the 522d Field Artillery Battalion and Cannon Company. The 232d Combat Engineers were also in close support. Now the 100/442 occupied the high ground. From Luciana, they could oversee and command the network of roads and communications emanating from Livorno.

On the 18th, the 3d Battalion took Colle Salvetti, the last high ground south of the Arno River. The following week, the 100th, under control of the Fifth Army, moved into Livorno and were deployed as security guards. On the 20th, the 2d and 3d battalions took Pisa, and were relieved and closed into an assembly area two days later near Colle Salvetti. On the 24th, the 2d and 3d battalions moved on to Vada and were joined by the 100th.

In three weeks of combat, from July 1 to July 22, the 100/442 melded into a fighting unit. The 100th and the 2d and 3d battalions came of age. They became a Regimental Combat Team. As such, they moved the enemy from the Cecina River area to the Arno River, liberated over a dozen towns, and held the key cities of Livorno and Pisa.

● *The medics were organized into a medical detachment and of course they were split into different units serving different battalions and they were assigned all the way down to the companies and we had medics assigned to the platoons of rifle companies. Anyway, these people were fantastic because when they got a call on the line in combat when people were getting hit and killed all over the place whenever there was a call for medic, they unhesitatingly got up and ran out and patched and took care of the wounded. I think this is one of the things that kept the morale of the unit up because we knew that no matter what happened, when we got hurt, the medics would be there to take care of us.*

Top left, 105mm howitzer gives support fire in the battle for Livorno — gunner is Cpl Edward Nakamura, cannoneer is PFC George Tanna, both from Hawaii. Top center, 100th patrols Livorno streets via jeep. Right, moving into the center of Livorno on a 6x6 truck. Bottom left, "Anybody interested in a slightly used SS (Schutz Staffel) Mercedes Benz?" Bottom center, the 10-minute break after marching into Livorno. Bottom right, favorite supply train to the hills of Luciana and beyond, T/5 William Hirata, Sardinian mule, and a Partigiano (Italian partisan)

59

• *It was on Hill 140 that T/Sgt Ted Tanouye, K Company, waged a one-man war on the enemy. Even to his battle-hardened comrades, it was unbelievable.*

T/Sgt Tanouye spotted a machine gun nest with its gunners getting ready to open up. He fired first with his Tommy gun, killing three, causing others to run away. Up the hill, a German with a Schmeisser machine-pistol ripped away at him. He missed, but T/Sgt Tanouye did not. His Tommy gun hit him and three other Germans. T/Sgt Tanouye moved up the hill to where the enemy was dug in. He opened fire on their trenches and was hit in the left arm by a grenade fragment. T/Sgt Tanouye continued to fire into the trenches, holding his Tommy gun in his right arm. Running out of ammo, he crawled to his left to his unit to get a fresh supply of ammo. Another German position opened up with machine pistols. T/Sgt Tanouye threw a grenade that shut it up permanently. Then he went back up the hill and attacked another machine-gun nest with his Tommy gun and wiped it out. Three of the enemy higher up on Hill 140 started shooting at him. They missed. He didn't and wounded all three. T/Sgt Tanouye then directed his men and joined them as they seized their objective. After setting up a defense perimeter to secure the area taken, T/Sgt Tanouye took time out to have his wound treated.

T/Sgt Ted Tanouye received the Distinguished Service Cross for this action. He later died of wounds received in action near Florence, Italy, along the Arno River.

• *It was sometime after Hill 140 that Ike Masaoka from our company got up to help a guy who hollered out for medic because he was hit. In doing so, Ike got hit pretty badly and, for a while, they thought they were going to lose him. He's pretty badly disabled; I think he's classified almost 100% disabled but he's functioning OK back home in Los Angeles. He's typical of the medics . . .*

Above, "no sweat" GIs heading for regimental reserve (a brief lull in combat). Above center, more GIs sweating out the "right card." Above right, PFC Charles Mimura, Hawaii, plays taps to honor the memory of the 72 fallen comrades from the 2d Bn. Below, Company K bivouac area. Below right, 100th passes in review in Livorno to receive the Presidential Unit Citation for outstanding action at Belvedere, Italy

● *Our house of ill repute met the specifications as prescribed by the Colonel. It was run by a sergeant who relished the idea. They had a building with one madame and four girls, good-looking girls. We had four bedrooms. It was a two-story house. I was in the parlor and the sergeant was outside the door. He had a Tommy gun, I had a Tommy gun, and we had a cash box and the madame stationed on the first floor. So we got three guards out there. Since the sergeant could speak Italian, he selected the girls. The girls were happy to come into the city to serve that purpose. We had no venereal disease all the time we were in Leghorn — the Pro Station was right next door.*

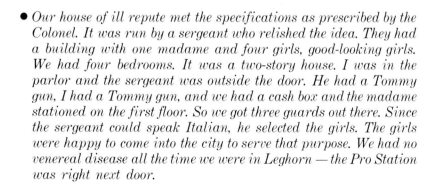

You don't know what's going to happen next. Even in that kind of fear I think the ones that really survive, especially mentally, were able to see humor in anything or try to see humor in things. Of course there was the eternal griping or bitching if you want to call it that. I guess bitching was a way to relieve your feelings more than anything else. I don't know how humorous you can call this, but in a way it is. Here we were sitting on a ridge and this was the 4th of July. It was a good morning and things were fairly calm. And I said a few of us was on this particular ridge when somebody remarked, "Sure is quiet for the 4th of July," and about the time the words died out, that's when the German artillery came in and gave us hell.

You work as a team . . . those guys from the islands taught me something I never ran into on the Mainland . . . you really have a buddy system. When you get into trouble you don't leave your buddy, ever, and he won't leave you, and this is a tremendous thing. You make it or you don't make it, together. But always together. So when you go into action, you know that if you get into trouble, your buddies are going to stick with you. They're not going to leave you hung up out there alone. The medics are going to get you if you get hit. If you get into a tight spot, everybody pitches in to get you out. You're never alone, and you know that. It keeps you going.

Watch the older guys, the ones who have seen action. Try to copy their moves. There are some general rules — don't fasten the chin strap on your helmet. An explosion could blow your helmet off and your head with it. Don't light a butt in the open or at night unless you are under cover. Better yet, don't smoke during the day. They might spot your smoke. Remember, it's not just you who's going to be blown away, it could be your buddies. Listen to the sound of Jerry rifle, grenade, machine pistol, and artillery. They have their own sound, different from ours. Even their tanks have a different sound. Know the different sounds. It could save your life. When you're on the line and you hole up for a while, start digging a slit trench or foxhole unless the noise will give you

away. A foxhole is about 3 feet in diameter and about 3½ feet deep. You can sit on your helmet and look around in a circle. It's better for fighting. When the barrage comes, you can duck your head in the hole. Slit trenches need be only as deep as needed to get you and your body below ground level in a prone position. They are faster to dig and easier to dig when the ground is hard. If you take over a Jerry trench, look out for boobytraps. It's usually safe if you just chased him out of there.

Above left, church services in Orciana, Italy, 24 hours after town was taken by the 100/442. Below left: T/4 Howard S. Sakura, Seattle, T/5 Edward T. Kamaya, Honolulu, PFC Ted N. Ohira, Kauai, PFC Calvin I. Yasuhara, Hilo, and unidentified PFC, at right, sing "Abide with Me" at Memorial Services in Cecina, Italy, July 1944. Above: Capt Young O. Kim, Los Angeles, Lt Gen Mark W. Clark and Undersecretary of War, Robert Patterson, review an Honor Guard of the 100/442 in Livorno

● *One of the platoon messengers had a watch that he regarded the same way I regarded my pipe and pouch, you know. He went to bed with it; he'd carry it with him wherever he went. His platoon leader on one occasion asked to borrow the watch. The messenger was very reluctant to let him have the watch, but he finally let him have it. The next morning, an artillery shell landed in the messenger's hole and killed him. Now you know when you hear of stories like this, you get a deeper belief that you better hold on to the practices that you've been holding on to and not change because the minute you change, something is going to happen to you.*

Sentry

In mid-July, 1944, Gen Mark Clark ordered the 100th to secure and guard Livorno (Italy), and to allow no one to enter without orders.

A lone Nisei private, no more than 5 feet tall, stood guard at his road post. Along came a long line of army trucks and stopped in front of the private on guard. A colonel stepped forward and said, "We are from the Engineer Corps. We are here to secure the port and make it ready for the ships. Let us through."

Said the private, "May I see your orders, sir?"
"I don't have orders. I must get through."
"Colonel, nobody gets through without orders."
"I can kill you right here and take my convoy on through."

*The private drew a line in the dusty road with his foot and said, "Colonel, you cross this line, you **make**."*
*"**Make?** What is **make?**"*
*"**Make** means you are dead."*
"We can take you, you are only one."
*"Cross the line and you **make**," said the private.*

The long truck convoy line remained halted while field telephones buzzed all the way up to Army command. Finally the message came back down to the colonel, "Return to your base and get your orders."

The repercussions of this incident did, indeed, go to the very top. Gen Mark Clark came to Livorno and said, "Bring that private to me." As the private marched forward, Gen Clark put his arm around the private's shoulder, and said to the newsman and to his staff, "I commend this soldier to you. I selected the 100th because I knew my orders would be carried out. I can depend on the 100th to successfully carry out any mission. I have absolute faith in every soldier in the 100th. This private is an example of that trust."

The Anti-Tank Co. and the Southern France Campaign

On July 15, 1944, the 442d's Anti-Tank Company was detached and sent to join the First Airborne Task Force south of Rome. After a brief training period, the Anti-Tank Company, led by Capt Louis A. Ferris, became an "instant" glider company, and took off. With newly acquired jeeps and heftier British six-pounders, the Anti-Tank Company on 15 August glided to a landing on the coast of southern France at Le Muy. The landings were rough. Ten men were injured, and 1 jeep and 1 trailer were wrecked. At Le Muy, they set up roadblocks in support of the 517th Parachute Regimental Combat Team, which had preceded them.

Two days later, they were relieved by elements of the 36th and 45th Divisions . . . then back into action. On 18 August, the Anti-Tank Company moved toward the Franco-Italian border and fought the enemy in his defenses around Col de Braus overlooking the border town

of Sospel, France. These were reduced by early September. On 11 October, the Anti-Tank Company went into rest, and would rejoin the Combat Team in time to assist in the "Lost Battalion" rescue yet to come.

● 6TH ARMY GROUP, FRANCE—*As the "tank-killers" that helped pave the way for many an Allied victory, an anti-tank company of the courageous 442d Japanese-American Infantry Regiment is biding its time in the French Alps along the Franco-Italian border until it can take another swipe at the enemy.*

Holding defensive positions in the towering Alps along Lt Gen Jacob L. Devers' 6th Army Group front, the anti-tank company could easily rest on its laurels — but it isn't. In some parts of the Vosges Mountains near the German border — where the snow and wooded terrain made tank warfare impossible — its men were pressed into service as litter bearers, ammunition and supply carriers, and even as front-line infantrymen. A similar situation exists in the French Alps, where these self-styled "tank-

killers" are contributing greatly in hazardous mountain warfare.

After the successful drive northward in Italy, the company was attached to an airborne task force for the invasion of Southern France. On D-day it was towed over the coast of France in two teams of 18 and 26 gliders, and released. Despite an unexpected dispersal of gliders in the landings, the first guns were placed ready for action in less than an hour. For two days it held its position until it was relieved by the seaborne divisions which pushed inland and made contact.

Every member of the anti-tank company wears the Combat Infantryman's Badge for exemplary conduct under fire and the Glider Badge for action as gliderborne troops.

STARS AND STRIPES

R & R at Vada

The 100/442 had been pulled back to Vada for rest and rehabilitation on July 25. Two days later, Lt Gen Mark W. Clark, Commanding General of the 5th Army, presented the 100th with the Presidential Unit Citation for its outstanding military feat at Belvedere and commended the other units for their great accomplishments in the fight for Livorno. The following day, in a ceremony at Cecina, elements of the 2d Battalion formed part of the Guard of Honor for His Majesty, King George VI of England.

The first week of rest was one of great ceremony, but the second was one of deep tragedy. On August 2, the 109th Engineers of the 34th Division had just completed a demonstration of the recent developments in enemy mines and boobytraps for the 3d Battalion of the 442d. Most of the battalion had left for their bivouac area when the engineers started to reload their truck following the demonstration. A load of 15 to 20 varieties of mines — Tellers, S-mines, Schuh-mines, TNT blocks, detonators, and so forth — was being placed on the open platform of one of the GI trucks. And then it happened. The truck and men were blown 30 to 50 feet into the air. No one knows how it was triggered. In the tremendous explosion, 10 men were killed — 7 from the 109th Engineers, 2 from the 232d Engineers and 1 from M Company.

● *All in all, the regiment (442d) charged some 50 miles in four days . . . averaging as little as two hour's sleep a night, and were so far ahead of the supply lines they were without food for 24 hours.*

AP DISPATCH, JULY 1944

● *There were all kinds of boobytraps. Some were small and simple, some were large and complicated.*

The usual boobytrap was the trip wire kind. You would hit an unseen wire, the wire usually triggered a grenade.

This could be located near a latrine, along a path in the forest, or in a doorway or a stairway in a house. Anywhere.

Some of the more elaborate ones involved attaching TNT blocks (plastic charges) to trees that lined a road. As the troops moved down a row of trees along the road, the last tree would have a low wire strung across the road. The lead soldier would trip the wire and the trees would blow down on the column of soldiers following him.

A special boobytrap that the G.I.'s dreaded was the "nut-cracker." Three rifle rounds would be buried in the ground with a pressure-type detonator. It was devilish. Another had wires strung at neck height for personnel riding in jeeps. No explosives were needed. Just a strong wire, a speeding jeep, and you have a decapitated or seriously wounded crew. The army later welded a sturdy steel vertical bar to the front bumper. The bar had a notch at neck height to catch the wire and snap it.

Some of the guys said the Germans would take captured GI grenades, place them under a dead body with the pins pulled but with the trigger held down by the dead body. When the body was rolled over or lifted, the trigger would go off and in seconds, the grenade would go off. I never ran into a boobytrap like this.

● *We were never unnerved by Axis Sally. I don't know how she got the information. She had no prisoners of ours. Maybe she did get some; she must have, to know the regiment. She knew some of the hometown names and of course the names of the Islands. Still, we really enjoyed the American music. We weren't about to desert or give up even if she gave green stamps.*

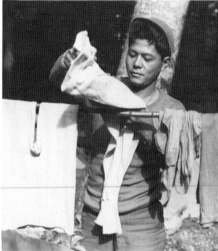

• *Their records in battle have been marked by one outstanding achievement after another. They have written a brilliant chapter in the history of American fighting men.*

LT GEN MARK W. CLARK
COMMANDING OFFICER, 5TH ARMY

• *The people at the replacement depots and in the hospital were astonished that anybody would go AWOL to get back to a unit, because if anything, 99% of the guys were trying to figure out ways to stay in the hospital or get shipped further back rather than shipped forward, and here the 100/442 men were actually going AWOL to get back to their unit.*

R & R

Far left, elements of 100/442 marching to reviewing area, Vada, Italy. Center top, PFC Bill Takaezu, Hawaii, takes in the laundry. Center bottom, winners on the line and in the ring, left, Roy Nakamine and Marshall Higa, both from Honolulu. Above, Company I gives a big "cheese" to the photographer. Left, the 100/442 favorite pin-up and USO girl, Jinx Falkenberg — WWII tennis and movie star.

Crossing the Arno River

On the 15th of August, the rest at Vada came to an end, and the 100th was now separated from the Combat Team and assigned to the 107th AAA Group, Task Force 45 of the IV Corps. Fifty miles to the east, the 442d was attached to II Corps 45th Division. Three days later, the 442d was relieved from the 45th and attached to the 88th. They say this was done to confuse "Axis Sally." Whether it did or not, it certainly confused the 100/442.

After the castling was completed, the 100th was in the Pisa sector and the 2d and 3d in a sector near Florence. The game plan called for the bulk of the Fifth Army to be grouped south of Florence for a strike at Futa Pass and Bologna while the British Eighth Army was scheduled to swing further east. The problem was how to keep this information from the enemy. The 100/442 was directed to divert the enemy by making a considerable show of strength. They were to patrol aggressively all along the front so that the enemy would be kept off balance, wondering where the next blow would fall. This was easy enough for the 2d and 3d Battalions to do as the enemy was to the north of the Arno River, although there were occasional pockets of German defenders south of the Arno. In the 100th sector, near Pisa, the wide bends of the Arno River left many German patrols active to the south of the Arno. The 100th spent the major portion of their time cleaning out these pockets.

The Arno River area was flat, crisscrossed with hedges and vineyards. This made patrolling extremely hazardous. On a mission to clear out an enemy base along the river, Capt Robert L. Hempstead, commanding officer of M Company, 3d Battalion, led a combined L, M and Cannon Company Task Force and wiped out one stronghold with cannon fire. As the Task Force

● *One night we were sent out on a special night patrol to reconnoiter a certain area and to stay there till we were relieved. We took off on the double from the company outpost. With only the given azimuth on our compass, we steered a straight course across an open field to our destination. We didn't check for mines or booby-traps but kept going till we reached our objective. We set up a perimeter defense, secured the area, then we were told to come back. On our way back, we decided to cut across the same open field that we had crossed earlier. When we got there, the 232d Combat Engineers had minesweepers sweeping the field and marking off a safe path with white tapes. When we saw this, our eyes bulged, our faces turned a greenish hue. Achtung minen!*

● *There were a lot of the normal kind of things any other group would go through. You know, the "Dear John" letter type. I had a guy, a pretty good sergeant, who got a Dear John letter and received a ring back from the girlfriend and all that. I had to keep my eye on him because every time he had a chance, he'd volunteer to go on patrol, and when you go on patrol, why you know, if you're lucky you come back. And it's not a one man patrol. Finally I told the guy, "Hey, I'll call you when I want you to go on patrol. You want to commit suicide, you do it on your own, but don't take the rest of the guys with you." He got the message.*

● *John said he was not going to come back. We tried to kid him out of it. We didn't like to talk about it. We did not like to talk like that before we went into action. But he just talked about it matter of factly. As we listened, we just somehow knew he was going to get killed. We tried to kid him out of it, and we did the best we could. We were trying to find a way to keep him back but he didn't want to hang back. He was like meeting destiny or something like that. He went up and while trying to do his job, he was killed. He was too good a soldier to lose.*

Top left, Jitsuo Kobayashi, holding shovel, takes a break while James Ishimoto and Wallace Higa, all from Hawaii, check mortar base plate. Above left, with rifle at ready is Pvt Yeikichi Arakaki from Kauai. A sniper is hiding in the brush near the crest of the hill. August 1944. Right, S/Sgt Mamoru Masuda, C Battery, 522d Field Artillery Bn, directs supporting fire in the Arno River sector

moved past San Columbano, they were caught in machine-gun crossfire. Capt Hempstead opened fire with his Tommy gun (Thompson submachine gun) to draw attention to himself. He bought time for his men to find cover but lost his own life. The Task Force had several wounded. Capt Hempstead was awarded the Silver Star posthumously. The enemy base was knocked out by Capt Hempstead's patrol. The Nazis had 8 men killed in action and several wounded. The Task Force had one man dead and several wounded. Under a flag of truce, Chaplain Masao Yamada and S/Sgt Jimmie Kanaya from the 3d Battalion led the "medics" in full view of the enemy to treat the wounded. The enemy held their fire. The enemy medic also came out under his flag of truce. Chaplain Yamada and Sgt Kanaya exchanged words with the enemy aid man and learned that Lt Ralph Potter, who was wounded, had been taken prisoner.

The following day, Chaplain Yamada, again under the Geneva flag, went out and removed the dead. On other occasions, the medics had been fired upon, but this never deterred them from their duty. This devotion, this display of "go for broke" morale by the medics and by chaplains who cared for the men in the thick of battle, was one of the forces that fused the men into a fighting unit — they knew they would not be abandoned.

Town's secure, street's safe — take ten, then off again!

Platoon Leader Lt Charles Coyne, Boston, lights it up for Sgt Nakoto Taguchi, Kauai. No "chicken" in the combat zone

Left, S/Sgt Arata Kimura, San Jose, aerial observer for the 522d Field Artillery Battalion, confers with pilot, Lt Joseph C. Polancii

● *We had a chaplain in the 3d Battalion that "walked with God, hand in hand." He was Chaplain Masao Yamada from Hawaii. Chaplain Yamada cheated death on two occasions. First, when he accompanied the battalion graves registration officer to pick up bodies of men killed while on patrol near the Arno River. He was riding in the front seat of a jeep that veered off the road — the jeep detonated a mine. The mine blew the jeep 30 feet in the air. Chaplain Yamada was thrown out of the jeep; the driver and the grave registration officer were killed. Except for a slight concussion, Chaplain Yamada was unscathed.*

The second incident took place when he was holed up in an abandoned Italian house. While he was there the German artillery made a direct hit on the house, but fortunately the shell just passed through the walls of the building without exploding. Chaplain Yamada received a scratch on his hand from the falling debris.

● *The engineers are supposed to clear minefields but when you're in combat, sometimes the riflemen have to handle 'em. If you can't go around the mines, follow the guy in front of you. Walk in his footsteps. If you're the lead, and you have time, flop face down on the ground, inch forward prone (distributing your weight lessens the pressure, mines are pressure sensitive) and probe with your bayonet in the ground in front of you. If you tap a mine, place a marker in the spot (usually toilet paper around a rock), sidle off to the side and keep inching and probing. The guys that follow usually walk and avoid the paper, following your path.*

Teller or plate mines were planted by the retreating Germans usually in roads or shallow creek crossings where jeeps, trucks, or tanks would have to cross. Their weight would detonate the mine. The Germans also had an anti-personnel mine called the S-mine or "Bouncing Betty." Usually it was triggered by a trip wire. The mine would have an initial charge that would send it up in the air for about 3 feet where it would then blow apart and spread shrapnel in a 360-degree circle. It was very effective and much feared. There was very little protection against this type of mine. If you heard the familiar sound as it went up and if you were fast enough, all you could do was hit the ground flat as fast as you could and pray.

Another ingenious mine was the German "Schuh mine." Small, and made entirely of wood and powder, the mine was undetectable by the minesweepers. Placed along paths, and slightly buried, the "shoe-mine" was activated by the pressure of one foot. The mine had enough charge to maim and in some cases kill when stepped upon.

"Get Prisoners"

German PWs headed for the rear

Prisoners. Get Prisoners! G-2 sent out a call for prisoners so that they could be questioned for needed information about the enemy. The 100th in their sector had done their job. They had already taken some prisoners. The patrols from the 2d and 3d battalions made crossing after crossing of the Arno searching for prisoners without success. Finally, on 28 August 1944, a weary, exhausted K Company patrol, returning empty handed from an all-night foray, flushed four Germans just 150 yards from the 3d Battalion command post.

Like bananas, the prisoners started to come in bunches. The next night, a combined patrol from E and G Companies, 2d Battalion, grabbed five more prisoners. From the prisoners it was learned that the 2d and 3d battalions were facing the 71st Panzergrenadier Regiment. Later, the sound of Germans blowing up bridges and trees to create roadblocks was heard. Patrols and outposts and observation planes verified the data provided by the prisoners. The enemy was indeed pulling back to the Gothic Line.

The 100/442 relieved the British XIII Corps near Firenze. Here, a couple of the troops in an English "Dingo" command car. Italy, 1944

Winning the Rome-Arno Campaign

Upon learning of the enemy's withdrawal, the II Corps ordered a general advance. But even as the enemy withdrew, they fought an intense rearguard action. On September 1, a patrol composed of men from the 2d and 3d battalions crossed the Arno River under heavy enemy fire and established a bridgehead. F Company then moved through this bridgehead with an appreciated assist from tanks and from the 232d Combat Engineers to occupy Peretola. In the sector to the left, again against strong resistance, K Company crossed the Arno River. Guided through the minefield by Partisans, they finally moved into the town of San Mauro. On the same day, A and C Companies of the 100th spearheaded a drive across the Arno River in the Pisa sector. By 3 September, the 100th led a drive to the vicinity of Serchio River where they were delayed by strong enemy opposition. Three days later, the battle-weary men of the 100th in the Serchio River area and the 442d north of Florence were relieved, detached from their respective units, and sent south to Castiglioncello for rest and rehabilitation.

The 100/442's casualties in the Rome-Arno campaign totaled 1,272 — more than one fourth of their total strength. Of that number, 239 men were killed in action, 17 were missing in action, 972 were wounded in action and 44 received noncombat injuries. This is the price they paid for 40 miles of Italian countryside and for forcing the German army into retreat.

After four days of rest, the 100/442 headed for Naples and was assigned to the 7th Army. They were staged in the vicinity of Naples until 672 replacements, mostly mainlanders, arrived on September 18th. The replacements had one week in which to train and become integrated in their respective companies.

All types of armored vehicles surfaced during the Rome-Arno fighting. Here, Y.B. "Buddy" Mamiya takes over a decommissioned Italian tank

On the 26th and 27th of September, 1944, the Combat Team boarded Navy transports *Thurston, Dickman, Chase,* and *Henrico* and headed for Marseille.

Rhineland Campaign — Vosges

The 100/442d Regimental Combat Team landed in France at Marseille on 30 September 1944. They bivouacked about 10 miles inland, gathered their weapons for cleaning and their land legs for marching. On the third day, it started to rain. It seemed to rain or snow every day until they left for the Riviera almost two months later.

The 100th and the 2d battalions left the bivouac areas by truck to travel up the Rhone Valley to Charmois-devant-Bruyeres. The 3d Battalion journeyed by freight train — vintage World War I — on boxcars labelled "40 Hommes et 8 Chevaux." These little boxcars had four wheels and all were square. The "40" meant men, the "8" meant horses. From the fragrance, the former occupants must have been mostly the latter.

The 100/442 finally shook off the effects of the two-week journey by jarring truck and "40 & 8's" and re-grouped in an assembly area four kilometers west of Bruyeres. On 13 October they were attached to the 36th Division, Maj Gen John E. Dahlquist, commanding.

● *It was on the "40&8" train ride from Marseille to the staging area south of Bruyeres that the "C-Ration Caper" took place.*

We had been on a steady diet of K-rations while rattling up the Rhone Valley on this Toonerville Trolley of a train. We pulled into Lyons and stopped in the yards next to an open box car, and what do you know, it's full of C-rations, the canned food. PFC Rudy Tokiwa quickly organized a supply party and before you could say "all aboard," about 20 cases had been liberated. Then from out of nowhere, a colonel appears, screaming and shouting, "Put those cases back. You're all gonna get court-martialed."

Rudy kept his Tommy gun at ready as the "40&8" pulled out, and called back, "Sorry, these rations are for combat troops."

Top, the "40&8" that carried the 3d Bn of the 100/442 from Marseille to Charmois-devant-Bruyeres. October, 1944. Above, gourmet dining for a rifleman was a hot meal, any kind of a hot meal — in combat you ate K or Iron rations (raisin/chocolate)

Attack on Bruyeres

The "Glory Road" — moving up to Bruyeres

On 15 October, the attack on Bruyeres began. The 100th and the 2d battalions advanced abreast; the 3d was held in reserve.

The men did not know then that this was the beginning of a far different kind of fight than the ones waged in Italy. Here the battleground was close to the German border. In Italy, the Germans could afford to trade real estate for time, men, and materiel. Now the enemy had their backs to the wall. In the Bruyeres sec-tor, they were ordered to hold at all cost. Their fortifi-cations were deeper and more extensive, their fire power heavier and more intense, and their troops grimmer and more determined. They were ready to use every trick in the book of modern warfare, and they wrote the book — extensive planting of minefields and boobytraps; zeroing in of military targets (bridges, intersections, village squares, wells); heavy concentrations of artillery, rocket (screaming meemies — six-barrel rocket launchers), and mortar fire. They used tree-burst artillery shelling in the Vosges forest. They dug, fortified, and camouflaged machine gun nests in the underbrush of the forest — throwing back their cover like a trap-door spider and opening fire on the backs of passing troops. They were no longer the "hit-and-run" soldiers. They had no place to run. So they stayed to slug it out, and the 100/442 stayed with them.

Hills A, B, C and D lay to the north and west of Bruyeres and dominated the town. To take Bruyeres the high ground had to be cleared. Hill A was the objective for the 100th; Hill B, for the 2d Battalion. The hills were covered with pine forests. The valleys were open and clear — clear to the observing eyes of the enemy occupying the hills. As for the weather, it was again overcast with a cold, driving rain.

The men of the 100/442 knew that taking the hills would be a major operation. The Germans had the terrain advantage and were entrenched and determined to keep it that way.

Supporting the Combat Team were the 232d Combat Engineers, the 522d Field Artillery Battalion, Company B of the 752d Tank Battalion, Company C of the 363d Tank Destroyer Battalion, Company D of the 83d Chemical Mortar Battalion, the 36th Cavalry Reconnaissance Troop, and the 886th Medical Collecting Company. With friends like these, the 100/442 knew big troubles lay ahead.

The attack began at 0800 on 15 October 1944. The 100th and the 2d Battalion advanced about 300 yards and ran into stiff enemy resistance. Two hours later, they had penetrated 500 yards. Heavy enemy artillery and mortar and machine-gun fire checked their advance. Behind them a racket broke out. The two battalions had overrun four machine-gun nests in their advance. The 232d Engineers were fired upon as they cleared a roadblock. Several were wounded. The Engineers stopped

Far right, elements of 2d Bn, 100/442, moving up by truck to Bruyeres. Right, going over battle plans, 2d Lt Edward Androvette, 2d Lt Robert Foote, S/Sgt Min Shumida, and Sgt Minoru Ikehara, Company K, 3d Bn. Far right, bottom, bringing up supplies, jeep with heavy machine gun and vertical steel bar on bumper for cutting "neck" wires. Below, Capt Charles B. Feibleman working with Nisei crew to send 105's on a social call to the enemy

clearing and started fighting. Assisted by a rifle platoon from the 100th, the Engineers silenced all four machine-gun nests and resumed clearing the road.

This was the outcome of the Combat Team's first day of action in France: they had gained 500 yards and captured 20 prisoners (from the 19th Schutz Staffel, SS, Police Regiment and the 223d Grenadier Regiment). The 100/442 suffered 1 KIA and 20 WIA. This day proved to be a forerunner of events to come.

The next day the 100th and the 2d battalions resumed their attack and moved into the valley below Hills A and B. The enemy launched a counterattack in the 2d Battalion sector later that day. The Germans were supported by artillery, self-propelled guns, tanks, mortars, and heavy automatic arms fire. The 2d Battalion called the 522d Field Artillery Battalion and the 83d Chemical (Mortar) Battalion for support. Their accurate firepower helped check the counterattack, but it was not until the

● *Outside of Bruyeres, we were there for almost two weeks in the cold. It wasn't freezing but it was very close to it. It was raining all the time. When you slept on the ground, you slept in a puddle of water. In the morning that water would have a thin layer of ice. It was very close to freezing. It's raining all the time and you're in that kind of weather for two weeks. After a while every muscle of your body starts to tremble. I think that's a way of trying to heat itself. You can't talk without chattering, you can't hold anything without shaking. You see the muscles quivering under your skin. You're cold and you're sopping wet, and you've been sopping wet from the very first day. After a while, the fact that it's raining doesn't mean anything because you're so wet. Yet under those conditions nobody got sick, nobody got ill, nobody got pneumonia. Yet despite all the physical hardships, there was the constant terror of death, of people getting killed, mangled, or wounded. But again I say, it was sheer will power. When you come down to it, combat is really sheer will power.*

next morning that the last of the enemy elements were driven back by E and F companies.

But E and F companies were to have no respite; during the next hour, the Germans launched their second counterattack with two companies. Other elements of the 100th and the 2d joined the fray. There was a furious battle. Again the Germans were held off. Two hours later, the enemy mounted another attack, the third within 24 hours. The 100th and the 2d battalions held their ground. The 522d 105's and the 83d 4.2 mortars again exacted their toll. The enemy armor was routed this time by the 2d Battalion's "anti-tank squad" of six bazooka men!

The 100th and the 2d had received two early morning visits by the Germans. They now decided to return these. The fighting wasn't over yet. The 100th and the 2d moved down into the valley approaching Hills A and B. The Germans had transformed the few farmhouses in the plains into machine-gun nests. Now these had to be cleaned out. All during the day and into the next, the two battalions fought to clear a crossing through the valley to Hills A and B. On October 18, a TOT (time on target) barrage of 30 minutes was laid on the hills by five bat-

Above, moving into Bruyeres. Note tanks (ours); 752d Tank Bn, with 100/442 formed "gruesome twosome." They teamed up to give the Germans a very bad time. Below, Combat Team securing outskirts of Bruyeres. Top right, Nisei GIs moving by knocked-out Nazi half-track. German troops encountered at Bruyeres included 19th SS Police Regiment, 223d Grenadier Regiment, 736th Grenadier Regiment, Fortress Machine Gun Bn, 196th Fusilier Bn, and the 192d Panzer Grenadier Regiment

• *We were joined by the men of the 442d ... brave determined little men ... who seemed almost anxious for a fight. "Man, they could fight!" exclaimed a George Company wire man ... "They didn't appear scared of anything; they just kept advancing through the forest standing up and firing from the hip at anything that moved. They sure knew how to make our Tommy Gun talk!"*

141st INFANTRY REGIMENT
36th DIVISION

• *Combat is like walking into a completely dark room that you know is full of rattlesnakes. You don't know if you'll get bitten or not. But you're very scared and very careful.*

• *Before we went into action to liberate the town of Bruyeres and later rescue the "Lost Battalion," we submitted a requisition to the Quartermasters for raincoats, undershirts, shorts, socks, shoes and miscellaneous items of clothing and field equipment. The supplies caught up with us after we left the lines to go into division reserve for a brief rest. We were shocked and "pleasantly" embarrassed when we checked our newly arrived clothing supplies. The raincoats had hoods and the inside label read, "WACs." The other surprise came when we opened the bundle marked "shorts" — turned out to be "woman's unmentionables." Evidently Quartermasters couldn't find any size small enough to fit our men so that they substituted what they had on hand. The raincoats were handed out, but not the panties. We didn't want our men to be known as being "mahu" (gay).*

● *The 442d Regimental Combat Team . . .entered combat on October 15, 1944, as a unit of the 36th Division . . . engaging in the assault on Bruyeres, which was entered after three days of bitter fighting. The 7th Army report on these operations states, "Bruyeres will long be remembered, for it was the most viciously fought-for town we had encountered in our long march against the Germans. The enemy defended it house by house, giving up a yard only when it became so untenable they could no longer hope to hold it."*

GEN JACOB L. DEVERS

talions of artillery. The 3d Battalion was pulled from reserve. Their objective, along with that of units of the 143d Infantry Regiment, 36th Division: take Bruyeres. Even after the TOT barrage, it took over four hours of savage fighting for the 100th to take Hill A. The 2d Battalion battled for nearly seven hours to secure Hill B. The key hills commanding Bruyeres were now in friendly hands. The 3d Battalion and the 143d Infantry Regiment then commenced a house-by-house clean-up of the town.

The Battle for Bruyeres was characteristic of the Germans' "stand and fight" orders in France. They had thrown men and materiel into the defense of Bruyeres, but were unable to stop the drive of the 100/442. The Germans suffered approximately 130 casualties and lost another 134 as prisoners.

Far left, 100/442 marches through Bruyeres, liberated after three days of intensive fighting. Left, climbing hill east of Bruyeres after heavy artillery barrage (ours) — note shattered trees and fallen limbs. Above, looking west toward Bruyeres in the valley. Man on left carries a Tommy gun; center, a shovel off the left hip and a carbine off the right shoulder, what the well-dressed infantryman will wear

On the other side of the hill from Bruyeres . . . no surprises, Jerry waits for us at the bottom

On to La Broquaine

Two more hills fell to the 100/442 in rapid succession: Hill D to the 2d Battalion on October 19; Hill C, to the 100th on the 20th.

After the taking of Hill D, the 2d and 3d battalions moved a mile beyond, traversing a minefield en route. Their objective was the railway embankment near La Broquaine. Upon reaching the embankment, they learned the enemy had retaken Hill D. Companies F, H and L were sent back to deal with the infiltrating enemy force. The fighting was intense and the enemy was seem-

ingly entrenched. Then a small incident happened that changed the course of the battle.

One of the men in F Company was wounded and T/Sgt Abraham Ohama went to his aid. He was hit by enemy fire. The medics went to retrieve him and the other wounded man. They placed T/Sgt Ohama on the litter and were about to carry him back when the enemy opened fire again and killed Ohama on the stretcher. The F Company men were furious. What had been a stand-off fight now turned into a one-way onslaught.

F Company troops, acting as one, charged the enemy and routed them from their positions on Hill D. They killed 50 and captured 7. For F Company, Hill D will forever be Ohama's hill.

The 2d and 3d battalions were still held up on the railway embankment at La Broquaine. The Germans counterattacked across the railroad tracks with heavy artillery and tank support. Two of the tanks threatened to break through into G Company's sector. S/Sgt Yoshimi Fujiwara thought otherwise. Running defiantly into intense machine-gun fire, he knocked out one tank with a bazooka charge and forced the other to withdraw. For this action, S/Sgt Fujiwara received the Distinguished Service Cross.

In another skirmish, the enemy attacked a supply train, pinning down the supply party with machine-gun fire. S/Sgt Robert Kuroda of H Company moved forward and destroyed the machine-gun crew with a well-placed hand grenade. Next he opened fire with his rifle, killing

Cannon Company firing 105mm shells in support of the 100/442 as they push the Germans out of Bruyeres and into hills beyond

three more. S/Sgt Kuroda then went to the aid of an officer who had been wounded. Finding him dead, he picked up the fallen officer's Tommy gun and proceeded to blast the next machine-gun nest out of commission. As he turned to fire on the enemy riflemen around him, he was struck and killed by a volley of fire. S/Sgt Kuroda was awarded the Distinguished Service Cross posthumously.

83

Above, moving up, Vosges Forest. Right, combat zone, fighting from tree to tree.

Action at Belmont

During the same afternoon, an enemy armor column was spotted on the road from Belmont, moving toward the 2d Battalion's left flank. Armored Tank Force Felber was hastily organized by Col Pence, the Regimental Commander, and dispatched up the road to meet the column. But before Task Force Felber could engage the enemy, a Thunderbolt fighter squadron greeted the Germans. They scored seven direct hits, eliminating the enemy armored threat for good.

At 1710 that evening, after a 20-minute preparatory artillery barrage, the 2d and 3d Battalions attacked the Germans along the railroad embankment. The two battalions moved over the tracks and reached the edge of the Belmont woods where they were stopped by minefields and a hail of small-arms fire from the enemy positions. During this action, Company K obtained a complete set of enemy defense plans from the body of a dead German officer.

84

Acting on this information, the Regiment quickly formed the O'Connor Task Force, composed of Companies F and L and headed by 3d Battalion Executive Officer, Maj Emmet L. O'Connor. Under cover of darkness, the Task Force boldly penetrated deep into enemy territory and moved to the left flank in order to come up on the rear of enemy forces attacking the 2d and 3d Battalions. At dawn, the Task Force went to work. Lt Binotti, a forward observer from the 522d Field Artillery Battalion and a Task Force member, called pinpoint accurate fire. Some 80 of the enemy were killed. Caught in the pincers, the Germans fought obstinately, but by late afternoon October 21, the 2d and 3d Battalions had

● *Actually in the combat, you die many times . . . every second, every minute, you're there, I think you're afraid . . . you're afraid of lots of things that's going to happen because you are always in danger. There's no such a thing as safety. When everything happens, the barrage comes, then the enemy starts coming at you, or you start going after the enemy — you know you're going to get it one way or the other. Usually the percentage is against you because the enemy is waiting for you and you're trying to root them out and this is the whole thing. And, as I said, you got to get it sometime. But on this, you've really got to be lucky; fate has to be with you. Some of them will say the bullet has my name and all that, but I think if you're in the right place at the right time or if you're in the wrong place at the wrong time, you're going to get it.*

How we like to face the German 128 artillery piece . . . with M/Sgt Sam Katsumoto, Service Company, in charge. Right, medics bringing in the wounded

joined with elements of the O'Connor Task Force to close the jaws and send the surviving Germans in retreat up the road to Belmont.

La Broquaine and the Bois de Belmont were finally taken. The enemy lost 80 killed in action; 54 prisoners; and, in equipment and supplies, 3 ammo carriers, 1 anti-tank gun, and a large supply of small arms. The O'Connor Task Force suffered 2 casualties. Companies F and L each received the Presidential Unit Citation for this outstanding combat accomplishment.

● MANDAN, NORTH DAKOTA—*Lt Col James M. Hanley, commander of the famed 2d Battalion of the 442d (Japanese-American) Infantry Regiment, took time recently on the Western Front to write a letter to his home town editor, Charles F. Pierce of the Mandan Daily Pioneer.*

Col Hanley, son of James M. Hanley, Sr., of Mandan, took exception to a remark in Editor Pierce's column some weeks ago which read: "A squib in a paper makes the statement that there are some good Jap-Americans in this country but it didn't say where they were buried."

Col Hanley's letter, published in the Daily Pioneer on March 31, declared:

10 March 1945
Southern France

Dear Charlie:

Just received the Pioneer of Jan. 20 and noted the paragraph enclosed.

Yes, Charlie, I know where there are some GOOD Japanese Americans — there are some 5000 of them in this unit. They are American soldiers — and I know where some of them are buried. I wish I could show you some of them, Charlie. I remember one Japanese American. He was walking ahead of me in a forest in France. A German shell took the right side of his face off. I recall another boy, an 88 had been trying to get us for some time— finally got him. When they carried him out on a stretcher the bloody meat from the middle of the thighs hung down over the end of the stretcher and dragged in the dirt — the bone parts were gone.

I recall a sergeant — a Japanese American if you will — who had his back blown in two — what was he doing? Why, he was only lying on top of an officer who had been wounded, to protect him from shell fragments during a barrage.

I recall one of my boys who stopped a German counterattack single handed. He fired all his BAR ammunition, picked a German rifle, emptied that — used a German Luger pistol he had taken from a prisoner.

I wish I could tell you the number of Japanese Americans who have died in this unit alone.

I wish the boys in the "Lost Battalion" could tell you what they think of Japanese Americans.

I wish that all the troops we have fought beside could tell you what they know.

The marvel is, Charlie, that these boys fight at all — they are good soldiers in spite of the type of racial prejudice shown by your paragraph.

I know it makes a good joke — but it is the kind of joke that prejudice thrives upon. It shows a lack of faith in the American ideal. Our system is supposed to make good Americans out of anyone — it certainly has done it in the case of these boys.

You, the Hood River Legion post, Hearst and a few others make one wonder just what we are fighting for. I hope it isn't racial prejudice.

Come over here, Charlie, I'll show you where "some good Japanese Americans" are buried.

J.M. HANLEY,
HQ. 442d INF. APO 758

Biffontaine

While the 2d Battalion was kept in reserve, the 100th and the 3d Battalion picked up the attack to the east. The 100th seized the high ground above Biffontaine, cut the Belmont-Biffontaine road, and forced the Germans out of Belmont. The 3d Battalion protected the 100th's left flank and moved northeast, clearing out pockets of sporadic enemy resistance. Artillery fire continued to fall.

But the Germans did not retreat. They counterattacked! They hit back at the 100th positions overlooking Biffontaine. They poured in fire from artillery, *nebelwerferen* (rockets), and even fire from anti-aircraft guns. The 100th dug in and held their ground, but ammo and food began to run low. Supplies were being moved up with protection from five light tanks and a platoon from A Company when . . . wham! Fifty Germans ambushed the supply train.

S/Sgt Itsumu Sasaoka, Company A, riding atop a tank, was badly wounded, but quickly opened fire on the enemy with the tank machine gun. He saved the platoon

---

● *After we had been awarded the combat infantryman's badge we were given 10 bucks a month extra because of the fact that we had a combat infantryman's badge. But those of us in the rifle company felt pretty bad because the combat medic who suffered along with us got a medic's badge but he didn't get a nickel extra for it. So it was a routine thing for us to chip in into the helmet every month when we got our pay and give a little spending money to the medic who took care of us. Bless his soul, ol' Sadao Sakamoto our medic, every time he went on leave he would use the money that he had collected and come back with bottles of cognac for us. But that's the way it was. We felt very strongly about the medics having equal recognition and rewards.*

German Morder III Tank Destroyer mounted a high-velocity 75mm gun that took a heavy toll of Allied positions and tanks

from certain massacre and enabled the other tanks to escape. Then, exhausted from his wounds, S/Sgt Sasaoka fell from the tank. He was reported missing in action. For his heroism, S/Sgt Sasaoka was awarded the Distinguished Service Cross.

The steep terrain prevented the tank supply trains from reaching the 100th. Finally, a foot-supply party from G and L companies succeeded in reaching the 100th with the much-needed supplies.

The Bicycle Battle

Even as the 100th was moving along the high ground overlooking Biffontaine, a special detachment of German bicycle troops attacked along the right rear flank. To counter this move, the 2d Battalion was quickly pulled from reserve and thrown into the fire-fight. The bicycle troops were rolled back. The 2d Battalion had beaten off an attack by a mobile unit!

The 100th was now able to move into Biffontaine, but it took two days of house-to-house fighting to convince the enemy that the 100th had come to stay. Soon after the Nisei entered Biffontaine, the Germans counterattacked. The fight raged for three hours. The Germans stopped briefly to regroup, then returned with tanks. Their counterattack lasted all afternoon. A German tank would pound a house to rubble. The men of the 100th would huddle in the cellar. When the tank stopped firing, the enemy infantry would move in. Then the 100th came out of the cellars and fought over the rubble to stop the enemy. The 100th held.

The supply route into Biffontaine was tenuous to nonexistent. On one occasion, a carrying party led by Lt Jimmie Kanaya was taking 20 wounded and some captured Germans to the rear when they were set upon by a superior enemy force. Only two men escaped. Capt Young Oak Kim, severely wounded, and T/4 Richard Chinen (medic) fled into the woods. The other 18 were taken prisoners.

On the second day, the Germans made their third and final attempt to retake Biffontaine. They mounted a bayonet charge, but failed to penetrate the 100th's first line of defense, and were forced to retreat. Biffontaine remained in the hands of the 100th. The cost for the 100th: 21 killed in action; 122 wounded in action; and 18 captured. For the Germans: 40 killed in action or wounded and 40 more taken prisoners. In materiel, the enemy lost: 1 ammo carrier; 1 recon car; 2 ambulances; 3 command cars; 2 anti-tank guns; 6 machine pistols; 100 rifles; 7 radios; and 3 switchboards.

On October 23 and 24, 1944, the 100th, 2d and 3d Battalions were ordered back to Belmont to rest. It was much needed. They had spent eight days in grueling combat, had fought the enemy in rain and fog, from foxhole to foxhole, knee-deep in icy water. The enemy seemed to have an endless supply of artillery and mortar shells with determination to match. In reality, it was an enemy whose back was to the wall.

Rest in Belmont was brief and intermittent — as intermittent as the artillery fire that fell on the main road junction in Belmont. But it was rest, and two days of it were better than none. It felt good to take a hot bath and get into dry clothes again.

A carrying party, similar to one below, was taking 20 wounded to rear when set upon by a superior force of Germans

The "Lost Battalion"

On 25 October 1944, the rest came to an abrupt end. The 2d Battalion of the 100/442 went into action relieving the battered 3d Battalion of the 141st Regiment of the 36th Division. On taking over, the 2d Battalion proceeded to advance some 200 yards before running into intense enemy fire. The 2d dug in and fought off attacks from the front and from the flanks. The Germans were trying to encircle them and pinch them off. But for the 100/442, it was a day like any other day. That afternoon, the 100th and the 3d Battalion moved up to protect the

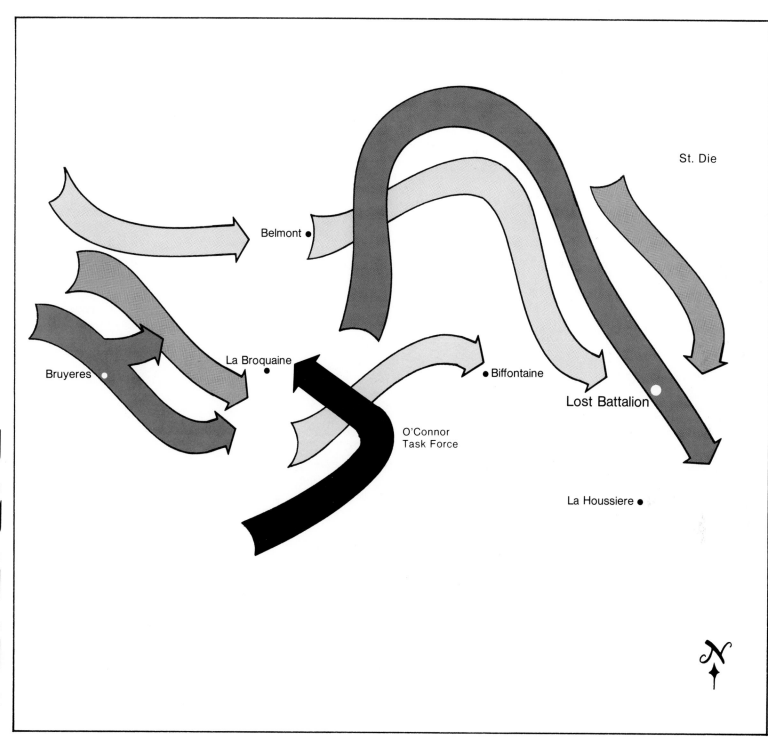

St. Die

Belmont •

La Broquaine •

Bruyeres ○

Biffontaine •

Lost Battalion ○

O'Connor
Task Force

La Houssiere •

100th Battalion

2d Battalion

3d Battalion

O'Connor Task Force
Co. L & F

flanks of the 2d Battalion. When the 100/442 received their orders, they got the full story — for the past two days, the 1st Battalion of the 141st Regiment had been cut off nine miles down the "road." The 2d and 3d Battalions of the 141st had made several attempts to reach their 1st Battalion, but had been beaten back. Now the 100/442 were ordered: "Reach the 'Lost Battalion.' "

The Combat Team moved out at 0400 in pitch black darkness with battalions abreast. They had, in support, attached: Companies B and D, the 752d Tank Battalion; Company C, 3d Chemical Mortar Battalion (4.2 mortars); Company D, 83d Chemical (4.2) Battalion; Company C, 636th Tank Destroyer Battalion; the 133d Field Artillery Battalion; and their own 522d Field Artillery Battalion and Cannon Company. Again, the 100/442, surrounded by such good and boisterous friends, knew they were headed for another "bust."

The battalions advanced slowly against heavy small arms and mortar fire. At 1530, 27 October, the enemy struck hard at the 3d Battalion, moving down the center of the battalions. I and K companies bore the brunt of the attack. A Mark IV tank and a half track supported by infantry blocked K Company's advance. The men

dug in and fought back. They held their ground but the tank was able to pivot and, with its wide-ranging cannon, pound the defensive positions. The situation became serious. PFC Masuichi Yogi of Company K, despite heavy small arms and automatic weapons fire, crawled within 25 yards of the tank. He knelt in full view of the enemy. He calmly fired his bazooka and scored a direct hit, knocking the tank out of commission. Two German bazooka men tried to zero in on PFC Yogi, but PFC Katsuotoshi "Pop" Sano quickly inserted another round in the bazooka and PFC Yogi fired first, killing one of the Germans. The other fled back into the forest. PFC Yogi, killed in a later action, was awarded the Distinguished Service Cross posthumously for this action.

The German tank, now a disabled heap with bogie wheels blown, was no longer a threat. The enemy counterattack had faltered. The next morning, 28 October, the Combat Team moved out once again. Still the enemy continued to fight back with a savage display of artillery and "screaming meemies" fire.

On the right flank, the 100th Battalion chased the Germans across a draw and onto the next hill. It was a trap. On following the enemy through the draw, the

---

● *We had been fighting and had broken through to Bruyeres and now we were pulled back for a rest. This was about the 25th of October 1944. After two days' rest, we were notified on the 27th that we had to reach the "Lost Battalion," the First Battalion of the 141st Regiment of the 36th Division. They were stuck out there on a point. They had 275 men out there about nine miles in Jerryland near St. Die. The flanks couldn't catch up with them so there they were. The Germans had circled them. Other troops tried to break through but couldn't. Airplanes had dropped food and ammo but the food and ammo kept rolling down the hills, into the trees, or into German hands. Our men were in a bad way. They'd been out there for a week, and that's when we were called in. They*

had 275 men when they started and, of course, we had our regiment when we moved in.

From the very first day until we reached them, it seemed like an eternity. It couldn't have been more than a week. We lost officers and men right and left every day. We lost so many men you couldn't count. I was the acting 1st Sgt for Company K. My pencil was worn down to a stub trying to keep track of the people we lost. We kept asking for replacements. None came up. We were lucky to get just food and ammo. Nothing could come up through that tremendous barrage that the Germans put down on both sides of us, it was like going through a narrow corridor with the enemy on your right and left, laying down a barrage of mortars, small arms

The enemy had excellent tanks, like the Mark V Panther shown at top left. Both sides used tanks at the outset of the drive to reach the "Lost Battalion" but usage declined as the troops moved deeper into the dense forest and the terrain worsened

fire, artillery, everything. And we were working through a forest. This was the Vosges forest. The underbrush was enough for the Germans to set up "trap-door" spider (hidden) machine-gun nests and so forth. When we bypassed them, they would open up their guns behind us. We ran into all kinds of stuff like that.

It was raining at first and by the time we reached the "Lost Battalion," it started to snow. It was always cold. We had trench foot. A lot of cases of it. The orders were, "If you can walk, you don't go back," because we were so low on men. It was terrible because trench foot is nothing like athlete's foot. You could lose a leg. But we couldn't spare the men and so if they could move around and pull a trigger, they had to stay and fight.

There was no thought of turning back. Never. We didn't think about turning back. No one even mentioned it. We just kept plowing forward to reach the "Lost Battalion," period. That was our goal and that's where we were headed. We knew that the 100th was guarding the flank. Every inch or yard of ground that we gained during the day, the 100th would fill up along the flank. It was a narrow path but we knew the 100th was guarding it. It was rough but we knew we were okay. We just kept plowing ahead and so this little thin line was kept open. We would send people back for supplies and ammo and they would get hit and killed. The last team I sent, the night before the rescue, about five guys went back for ammo and supplies — three of them were hit.

Forward aid station operated by medics of the 2d and 3d Bn, 100/442, Belmont, France, October 1944

100th was caught in an hour-long artillery barrage — treetop bursts that wounded 20 men. But the 100th refused to relinquish their ground on the right flank. They dug in.

The 3d Battalion went down the middle of the ridge. And as the saying goes, "it was down and dirty." The men quickly ran into the first of three heavily entrenched and fortified ridge barriers. The first one was a true anti-tank barrier manned by a company of infantry with a heavy complement of automatic firepower. Company K banged head-on into the first roadblock and after intense fighting, knocked out two machine-gun nests. Aided by the accurate firepower of the 105mm Howitzers from 522d Field Artillery and Cannon Company, they eliminated the third barrier. Then the 3d Battalion was able to advance about 500 yards before the enemy regrouped and set up a withering barrage of interlocking

automatic fire. The 3d dug in and held the ground they had won.

The 2d Battalion had a better go of it. Lt Col James M. Hanley, Commander of the 2d Battalion, attacked Hill 617 from the west. G Company was to attack frontally, and was spread thin to simulate a battalion. Col Hanley circled his other two companies behind the enemy on Hill 617. Their luck held. Undetected, they were able to move into position that night, and waited for dawn to attack.

The enemy was determined to stop the 100/442 from rescuing the "Lost Battalion." Fresh troops from the Germans' 202d Mountain Battalion, the 198th Fusilier Battalion, the 933d Infantry Regiment and the 338th Infantry Division were all thrown into the fight.

Equally determined to effect the rescue was the commander of the 36th Division, Maj Gen John E. Dahlquist. On 28 October, he personally ordered the 100/442 to make contact at all cost. The "Lost Battalion's" situation had become desperate. Their airdrops were hanging up in the trees or rolling down the steep slopes of the ridge on which they were trapped. Some of the drops were recovered, but not many. The "Lost Battalion" was low on ammo, food, water, and medical supplies. They had wounded men who had to be evacuated and treated. To conserve their meager supplies, they pooled their ammo, their food, and their drinking water.

On the 29th, the 100th and the 3d Battalion, with tank artillery, rocket and mortar fire in support, moved out along the ridge toward the "Lost Battalion." The ridge was wide enough for only I and K companies of the 3d Battalion. The 100th was strung along the right flank but encountered a minefield and had to make a wide sweep to avoid it. The 2d Battalion, on the left rear flank, was busy clearing out Hill 617. The 3d had no options. They had to move directly on line where the Germans were waiting for them.

Lt Col Alfred Pursall, commanding the 3d Battalion, joined I and K companies when they were held up at the first barrier. A flanking attack was attempted, but after an intense firefight, the Germans remained entrenched. Lt Col Pursall then called for tank support fire in a second assault on the ridge block. The Germans stubbornly refused to be dislodged. A third attack was then launched. This time I and K companies, with Lt Col Pursall as point, rose as one from cover and moved into the enemy fire. The charge was not a dashing, yelling affair. It had an eerie, electrical quality, the men moving forward in a steady, relentless thrust as if acknowledging that this was the final one. The companies were running low on men and ammunition. The assault had to succeed. It did. The third attack battered down the German barrier and drove them back. The fighting was

hand-to-hand, head-to-head, tree-to-tree, an inferno of grenade and small-arms fire. I Company losses were 5 men killed and 40 wounded; K Company losses were identical. All officers were gone. Sporadic artillery and rocket fire continued to plague the area even after the enemy retreated.

On the right flank, the 100th moved northeast of Biffontaine, then turned right into a heavily wooded area skirting the Biffontaine/La Houssiere valley, which was defended by deeply entrenched and camouflaged enemy machine-gun nests and troop positions. Total advance for the first day: 700 feet.

The next day, the 100th pushed into the intense interlocking automatic gunfire and against the heavy concentration of artillery, rocket, and mortar fire only to run into the first of nine heavily sown minefields! That night, the 232d Combat Engineers cleared a path through the fields for the troops to advance. Braving another barrage of tree bursts from artillery, rockets, and mortars, the 100th advanced a thousand yards when they ran into yet another enemy barrier bristling

GI operates machine gun during battle for "Lost Battalion"

GI holds an M-1 Rifle, wt. 9.3 lbs. and worth its weight in gold. Nearby, an M-10 Tank Destroyer goes rumbling and whining by. Right, 142d Regiment GI relieves 100/442 "bazooka man"

● *But, the minute we find out we're in alert and we're going to hit the frontline, everybody wants to go to church. I think they want that extra protection or something to believe in that they're going to come through. And, I think every G.I. has something that they, or, myself, I was carrying a four-leaf clover that I found in Caserta. When I got off in Naples, I dropped my duffel bag and when I looked down, there's a four-leaf clover looking right at me. I told my friends that this is the thing that is going to bring me through the war. I believed in it and here I am today.*

● *We had been on the line for a week or so, so they decided to pull us off and give us a rest. No sooner were we allowed a shower and clean clothes, when the word got around that we were alerted. So everybody was questioning, how come? They said we were going to get a rest, but we were alerted on the second day. So the word got around that a battalion was trapped somewhere out there. So, that night we were on alert and we had to pack again. Then we moved out in total dark. I didn't know which way we were going, but we found a human chain to hold onto. I guess somebody knew the trail to the front line. The 3d Battalion took the center part of the assault. We were the assault battalion. The fire fight was almost continuous, everyday. They had the "Lost Battalion" really surrounded, and my platoon was cut down. We first lost our platoon leader, next our platoon sergeant, then our squad leader, finally the assistant squad leader. It ended up I was sitting around all by myself. I didn't know who was who, all I knew was I belong to I Company and we're assaulting. On the second day, Gen Dahlquist of the 36th and his aide came up to the front. They passed me and went to the right. I think K Company was on the right and he went down there. But, when I saw him come back, he had a bloody hand . . . I knew something happened. I didn't see his Lieutenant so I thought oh, oh, his aide got shot. Sure enough, that was it. So, eventually, this area turns out to be the Banzai Hill for I Company . . . it's a little knoll, but I couldn't see any Germans. The tank men could see them through their periscopes. They always tell me . . . "There's a machine gun right in front of you!" Well I could never see them because the Vosges forest is so thick. I think, actually our fighting was like Indian fighting. You never know if the enemy is going to be 10 feet, or 50 feet, or if he's going to be right behind you. You jump from one tree to another and keep on going. Well, this hill was taken by I Company, I think it was a 2d Battalion fellow, Akiyama, from Oakland, he and his buddy were shot on the top of the knoll by a sniper. Akiyama had gone after this fellow who had been hit because he had a tommy gun and he wanted his tommy gun. As he picked up the tommy gun, the sniper took another shot, grazed his forearm and forehead and, boom, he goes down. No, he didn't die. After the war I saw him, I saw that scar. I asked him, "I bet you I know where you got that scar — from Banzai Hill," and he says "Yeah." He says I was the third man to come up, the first guy was already dead. To* this day, I can't explain why this sniper took two men right off the same spot and he didn't shoot me.

Somebody hollered, "Tanks!" and we thought all the German tanks were coming. They had the tanks up there, too. So, here we had this knoll taken and we had to pull back. Then we had to take it over again. So that was our Banzai Hill. K Company had their Banzai Hill and L Company had another Banzai Hill. One man leads and the rest of them just go. And that's the only way, I guess, to take a hill.

Right after I Company took Banzai Hill, we made contact with the "Lost Battalion." Tak Senzaki was one of the few platoon sergeants we had left. I Company still had Capt Joseph Byrne. I asked him, "How come we didn't barrage Banzai Hill?" He says, "We couldn't because we were too close and we might hit our own men." So we had to take the hill by a frontal assault. I ended up with 8 men reaching "Lost Battalion." Right after we hit the "Lost Battalion," Capt Byrne got killed. One of his runners tripped a bouncing Betty, S-mine, and, instead of the runner getting it, Capt Byrne took the brunt. When we reached the "Lost Battalion," there wasn't much time for rejoicing because we had to go right past the other side of the "Lost Battalion," dig in and set up a perimeter defense.

The Vosges was the most savage battle that I was ever in. You never saw the enemy, or, if you did see him, it was in close combat. And, if you got hit, the chance of survival was less because of the cold. The wounded would go into shock very quickly. I think it was really a mess compared to other battles.

- During the drive to rescue the "Lost Battalion," Capt Joseph Byrne grabbed a BAR (Browning Automatic Rifle) from one of his fallen comrades and personally led a charge up Banzai Hill with his company. His men, inspired by their towering 6′3″ captain, charged and took the hill. Capt Byrne, who was later killed by an anti-personnel mine, was awarded the Silver Star for this action.

After the "Lost Battalion" operation, the men of I Company chipped in and had a loving cup made in honor and memory of their late company commander, Capt Joseph Byrne.

The Silver Star and the memorial cup were sent to his older brother, Lt Col Byrne, a West Pointer.

- I remember one night, it sounds gruesome, but it's true. The fighting slowed down that one evening. I sat down. We were trying to count heads and a T/4 (sgt) came up and sat down. I sat on a helmet. He sat on one of the enemy dead. Now that's terrible. But there, in combat, we didn't give a damn. We were tired. The enemy was stiff, you know. We figured he was out of it, well whatever it was, it was over for him, so he sat on him. I started eating my K ration and he started eating his K ration. You reach a certain low point of sensitivity, you just don't give a damn. This was war. This was terrible. You're fighting so damn hard and you just keep going, and small things don't bother you after a while — like dead bodies.

with firepower. Only a frontal attack was possible now. There was no room on the ridge to maneuver; there was no time to make a long flanking attack around a minefield. Quickly Company B shifted one of their two remaining officers over to officerless Company C. Then they attacked. The fighting was as bitter and savage as any that they had encountered in all their previous months of fighting.

While the 100th and the 3d were crunching it out in the center and on the right flank, the 2d Battalion was having a field day. Its E and F Companies, having circled behind the enemy on Hill 617, attacked at dawn. This assault from an unexpected quarter caught the enemy completely by surprise. Those not driven down the front of Hill 617 into the frontal attack of G Company fled to the flanks in wild disorder. Hill 617 was quickly taken. The Germans suffered 100 killed in action and 41 taken prisoners by E and F Companies. G Company picked up another 20 prisoners as it moved up the slope.

On 30 October, I and K companies of the 3d Battalion and B and C of the 100th continued to move along the ridge that led to the "Lost Battalion." The 100th was securing the right flank and also establishing an all-important supply route to the forward companies. The 2d Battalion was moving up the left flank and cleaning out enemy pockets as they advanced.

Now it was I Company's turn. They ran into the last barrier manned by 50 German infantry. Elements of K Company moved over to assist. With "on-target" barrages by the 522d Field Artillery Battalion and the 83d 4.2 mortars, this roadblock was reduced, and I and K Companies continued the advance.

At 1400, an I Company platoon led by T/Sgt Takeo Senzaki broke through to the "Lost Battalion." At about the same time, K Company and B Company reached other elements of the "Lost Battalion." Shortly thereafter, the main units joined up. Their mission was accomplished. They had, against a formidable enemy, a forbidding terrain, and inclement weather, rescued the "Lost Battalion."

You fight as a squad or platoon — when you get hit, it's you, alone

● *The Germans started shooting medics in E (Easy) Company and this was Danny Inouye's company. They decided to shoot back at the German medics because they were killing our medics. There was a medic in Easy Company named Higuchi (Kelly) Kuwayama from New York, a Princeton graduate. I remember Kelly getting his platoon together and saying, "I'm an aid man, and they're shooting at me, and we're shooting at them, and it'll be keeping, it'll be going on." Kelly said, "You cannot fight evil with evil. Therefore I wish you would not shoot at their aid men." I remember Danny telling this story and saying that, "You know they all hung their heads in shame, and they didn't shoot back."*

Without the support of the 36th Division artillery and tanks and of its own 522d Artillery Battalion, Cannon Company, and 232d Engineers (who also fought as infantry), the mission would not have succeeded. It was a team effort — and it pushed the enemy back, mile after mile, despite his intense artillery, rocket fire and small arms fire.

The day after the "Lost Battalion" was contacted, I Company had only eight riflemen left with a sergeant in charge; all officers had been killed or wounded. K Company was in similar straits. They had 17 riflemen left with a sergeant in charge. They, too, had lost all their officers. The other companies suffered a similar fate. In all, over 800 casualties were suffered by the Combat Team in less than a week to effect the rescue of the "Lost Battalion." The "Lost Battalion," which originally numbered 275, was down to 211 men. They suffered 64 casualties. The Combat Team was not counting its losses. It was counting the enemy's. The enemy had lost nine miles of invaluable buffer land and the opportunity to eliminate a battalion of gallant, fighting men.

But the fighting was not over.

● *That evening, we called for replacements and waited to see if anyone would come up with additional ammo and food. They sent up a few replacements. They didn't get too many up. Shelling and everything was going along the path. They did send up an officer, a captain. This was K Company because we had no officers here. And we were down to 17 men as I mentioned ... several men came up, enlisted men. The Captain came to K Company's CP (my slit trench) and I briefed him and then I warned him about small arms fire out towards the front. He wanted to see for himself. I warned him not to go out there, but he was one of those officers who had to make sure everything was as stated and so he went out there and got killed.*

BAR (Browning Automatic Rifle) sticks its business end out of a camouflaged foxhole; Fox Company buddy checks for clearance

---

So I ran the company again that evening. The next morning I went up and counted heads to see how many we had left. We hadn't lost any men that night. Early that morning, it must have been about 0600, just as light was coming in that I woke the runner up. "Runner" is the guy that goes out like a messenger to check on the different positions ... I tell him to check the perimeter guards to make sure nothing had been breached or broken that night. He came back and said everything is standing. Then I was trying to get on the 300 radio to get some replacements and some supplies for the day when the shells started to come in. One hit the slit trench about 5 yards from where I was standing. This was the trench I was sleeping in the night before. The commo sarg, Robert Nitahara, was still in his slit trench about five yards away. The explosion buried his trench and knocked me down. I wasn't hit but I was sure he was. After much digging we got him uncovered. He didn't have a scratch on him. We were both lucky.

A half an hour later, a tree burst fragment rips my backside and another sergeant takes over Company K.

"We had to guard our water hole with machine guns because the Germans tried to pick us off when we came down for a drink . . . a whole combat patrol went out to try and make contact but only a few of us returned . . . they'd hit us from one flank and then the other, then from the front and the rear, but they never broke through . . . we never were so glad to see anyone as those fighting Japanese-Americans . . ."

Those drama-packed quotes came from the men of this war's "Lost Battalion" which was cut off from all friendly units for nearly seven days.

Some men broke into sobs early Monday evening when elements of a Japanese-American outfit cracked through the encircling enemy to effect the long-awaited relief.

The Japanese-American unit, fighting with fierce tenacity

Checking the morning report — how many men do we have left?

2d Bn men and officer preparing to move back into line, Vosges, November 1944

and dogged determination, started its move to rescue the battalion on the seventh day of entrapment.

Steadily they drove the enemy before them, using everything in the infantry book against the Nazis. Bayonet charges and close-in work with hand grenades took a high toll of German dead. One Japanese-American, for instance, killed six of the enemy by sniping with a captured rifle.

At another junction on the rescue trip, the Nazis yelled down from a hillside position: "C'mon and get us!" And the Japanese-Americans did exactly that, charging up with fixed bayonets and rifles fired from the hip. Few of those Nazis there ever saw the fatherland again.

Every officer in the trapped outfit was loud in his praise for the work of the Japanese-Americans, one phrasing it this way: "As fighting men, as real American soldiers, they are tops — absolutely tops."

PVT JOSEPH E. PALMER
BEACH HEAD NEWS

• *I was with the leading elements from K Company when we reached the "Lost Battalion." I was surprised. I was looking out for the enemy and here comes a guy out of a hole in the ground. I almost shot him but at the last minute I got a look at his uniform. His face looked grey green to me. I guess I would too if I were in a hole someplace for a week. I just stared at him and he stared at me. We really couldn't say much to each other. We advanced towards each other. I had lowered my rifle and he lowered his. And when we got close to each other, we just kind of looked at each other. But it was quiet. Then I guess I must have said, "Hi," or something stupid, and I guess I must have offered him a cigarette or something. Whatever I had 'cause I knew they were low on supplies. I guess I offered some K rations, whatever. After that first quiet minute the whole place erupted. "Hey, the 442 guys are here!" The guys started coming out of the ground like you don't believe. We didn't know that there were that many GI's out there. We had been pounding all alone up that deadly trail for days, finding nothing but Germans, gunfire, and barrages. Then all of a sudden we hear these guys, and there's no more fighting here. And they found they didn't have to fight 'cause we weren't Germans. We were numb at first and finally we realized that we were allies . . . you know it takes a little while for a simple thought like that to sink in after all the days of terror and the fighting. We were together and we were happy.*

• *The 442d Regimental Combat Team's most well-known exploit was the relief of the 'lost' 1st Battalion, 141st Infantry Regiment, of the 36th Division, which had been cut off by the enemy in the Vosges Mountains. In three days of savage fighting, with close combat use of the grenade and bayonet, the Nisei broke through the enemy cordon. In gratitude, the men of the 36th Division launched a drive and had all members of the 442d declared "honorary Texans" . . . this Nisei unit sustained 814 battle casualties (e.g., Company K was down to 17 riflemen; Company I, 8; there were no officers in either company the day after contact with the 'lost' battalion was made; sergeants were running the companies).*

U.S. CONGRESSIONAL RECORD

• *We rescued the "Lost Battalion" but the guys on the line knew it could have been us instead of them. The 100th was almost cut off in the fight for Biffontaine. Getting "lost" was part of the chances you took in combat. And that terrible feeling you get when you are cut off from your flanks or from supplies . . . the "Lost Battalion" guys, the 1st Battalion of the 141st Regiment of the 36th Division — they didn't give up when they got cut off nine miles into Jerryland. They "circled the wagons," pooled their ammo, food, and water, and held the Germans off for a week in spite of heavy artillery, "screaming meemies," mortar, and machine-gun fire. Try doing this for a week when the guys all around you are trying to butcher you. It takes a lot of guts, and the guys in the "Lost Battalion" weren't about to give up. "Lost?" I don't think so. Just a real tough situation and they hung in there.*

Hastily but well-constructed command post, Company F. Vosges, November 1944

Pushing the Enemy Off the Ridge

Heavy going — bringing up the 30-caliber, water-cooled machine gun

Again I and K companies, decimated or not, went on the offensive. Their new objective was to drive the enemy off the ridge. En route to the ridge they ran into a fourth and final barrier. Another intense firefight, a stalemate, a call for artillery and cannon fire; then another baptism by enemy small-arms fire. Again the enemy broke. The entire ridge was now under Combat Team control. Then the enemy counterattacked. I and K held fast. This time the Germans withdrew from the ridge for good. On 3 November 1944, the enemy was dug in on the forward slopes of the ridge.

The orders came down again! Move the enemy off the forward slope of the ridge. Once again, as the Germans poured in artillery and mortar fire and crisscrossed the area with grazing machine-gun fire, the Combat Team attacked. The ever-reliable 752d Tank Battalion came once again to the aid of 100/442. They came to the support of I, K and L in the center with F, G, and E on the flanks. The infantry and tanks teamed to drive the enemy from the slope. In three days of intense fighting, the men ran into everything the Germans could muster, but once again with excellent supporting fire from the 36th Division, they forced the enemy to retreat. On the 6th, some of the 232d Engineers stopped their day-and-night work maintaining the supply road to become "infantrymen" with the 100th. Each of the companies was down to 30 riflemen or less. The Combat Team had pushed the enemy off the slope, through the draw, up another hill, and were now driving him off yet another hill. M Company mortar fire was called upon to soften the hill. Two platoons of Anti-Tank Company joined F Company as infantry. By the 7th, the hill was cleared. The Combat Team dug in and held. During the next two days, the Germans dropped over 2,000 rounds of artillery on the 2d and 3d battalions to express their disapproval.

Now the 232d Engineers reverted to roadbuilding. For the next three days they were re-attached to the 111th Engineers to build much-needed corduroy roads that would carry supplies to the men at the front. If the Engineers weren't building, they were fighting, or clearing. They were always busy. They never seemed to wear out.

On 9 November 1944, the 100/442 was relieved from the front. They had helped shatter the enemy defenses and opened the way for the 36th to continue the drive that would eventually take them to the Rhineland. On the 10th, the 100th Infantry Battalion under 7th Army control was detached from the Combat Team and ordered south to the Maritime Alps.

In less than four weeks of fighting, 15 October to 9 November, from Bruyeres to St. Die, the Combat Team was down to less than half its regimental strength. The casualty list numbered almost 2,000. One hundred and forty men were killed; 1800 were in hospitals. I Company was now down to 4 riflemen! K Company managed to stay at 15 men during nine more days of fighting following the rescue of the "Lost Battalion." The Combat Team was more than ready for a long rest — they got four days!

Unbelievably, on 13 November, the Combat Team

● *One of my men asked me if I would have a burial service for his brother who was killed that day. I said all right. We got a truck and went down to Epinal. There were thousands of bodies there but we found the body. While we were standing by, some German prisoners who were helping with the grave registration offered to carry the body to the graveside. We refused because — well, I'm ashamed to say it, we hated the Germans so much — to think that a German who had killed this boy, who might have killed this boy, was going to touch his body again. So we refused, and we carried his body to the grave, to the graveside, and I had a service with the men. And after the service was over, I said "The Lord's Prayer" with the men, and the Germans standing by knelt down and also said "The Lord's Prayer" in German with me. "Unser Vater der im Himmel ist." I believe that's the German words for "Our Father who art in heaven." After the service was over, we got on the truck and on the way home I asked the sergeant, who was a young Christian boy, what he thought about the Germans saying "The Lord's Prayer" with us. He said, "You know, Chaplain, I was going to stand up, go over and push his face in . . . to think that he would say a prayer over the body of one he might have helped to kill." And then he said, "All of a sudden I realized that we were saying "Our Father" and not "My Father," not a Japanese father, not an American father, not a German father, but "Our Father," and the Germans were our brothers and we were fighting each other and killing each other. You know, Chaplain, for a minute there, I was ashamed that we, as brothers, were killing each other."*

H Company, 2d Bn, mortar crew sends 80mm message to Germans. St. Die, France, November 1944

was back in action, taking over defensive positions between the 36th Division and the 103d Division. Cannon Company gave fire support to the 2d Battalion and fired several thousand rounds at the enemy to dissuade him from doing anything so foolish as to mount a counterattack. The Germans did not attack, but the 2d and 3d did a lot of patrolling and reconnaissance as extra insurance. On the 17th, the regiment was finally relieved from its position in the Foret Dominiale du Champ, and the grimly intense fighting in central France came to an end.

The 100/442 had fought for a month. They had been cut down to less than half strength by enemy fire, but they took every objective asked of them. The 36th Division commanding general praised their accomplishments:

"The 36th Division regrets that the 442d Combat Team must be detached and sent on other duties. The period during which you have served, October 14 to November 18, 1944, was one of hard, intense fighting through ter-

rain as difficult as any army has ever encountered.

The courage, steadfastness, and willingness of your officers and men were equal to any ever displayed by United States troops.

Every officer and man of the Division joins me in our best personal regards and good wishes to every member of your command, and we hope that we may be honored again by having you as a member of our Division."

The Mediterranean Theater of Operations, United States Army publication, *442d Combat Team*, added this commendation:

"The month the Combat Team spent with the 36th Division had been a month of great heroism and great tragedy. At the time they went into the lines, these had been the only fresh troops the 7th Army possessed. The Nisei were committed against an enemy whose orders were to hold to the last man. In destroying the enemy, the Combat Team was so badly battered that it was impossible to go on without reinforcements, and these were not forthcoming. Perhaps if it had not been for the urgency of the mission to reach the "Lost Battalion," casualties would have been lower, but even this is doubtful . . . the Combat Team contributed mightily to the drive of the 7th Army when its contribution was needed most. That . . . is the highest accolade of any regiment of infantry."

● *Colonel Pence was a wonderful man. He was a lonely man, but he was a top colonel. He was promoted to general after the Vosges. He was fair, stuck by us, and backed us in everything we did. He had great faith in us. Nobody could say anything bad about Colonel Pence. He was a real leader and a soldier. For example, in Shelby, he said, "If the other troops pick on you, just get back at 'em, and don't take anything lying down." He was fair, and he trusted us. I think that's the answer to everything as far as General Pence is concerned.*

Above, men of the 100/442 pay their last respects to their fallen comrades at Armistice Day Ceremony, Bruyeres/Vosges/St. Die. 11 November 1944. Left: reading the scriptures, Chaplain (Capt) Hiroshi Higuchi; center, Lt Col Virgil R. Miller; and Lt Col James M. Hanley. Right, regimental commander, Col Charles W. Pence (Photo taken a week earlier while Combat Team was still on the line)

The Champagne Campaign

By 21 November 1944, all units of the 100/442 Regimental Combat Team had closed in at an assembly area near Nice, France, on the Riviera. The 100th arrived first and were ensconced in the choice spot, the Riviera sector; the 3d drew the central area, Sospel and environs; the

Above left, T/Sgt Tsutomu Samura handles the field telephone while 1st Lt Henry Oyasato looks for the enemy. French/Italian border, January 1945. Above center, S/Sgt Douglas Gusukuma with Tommy gun mans an outpost in the French alps. Right, the infantry (100/442) captures a two-man German submarine — doesn't everybody? Far right, church services high in the alps above Sospel attended by M Company. Backdrop is the imposing but ineffective "Maginot Line" fortification

● *One of the French collaborators had been raped and came to the medics. The doctor took care of her but was too busy to take her home.*

"Chaplain, will you take her home?" he asked. I said, "Yes." She was dressed in a flimsy nightgown and in no condition to walk. I carried her in my arms to her house. When we got there, I found a whole rifle company bivouacked in the house. The roof fell in. Nobody listened to my explanation.

● *The 442d Regimental Combat Team is probably the only infantry unit in history to capture an enemy submarine, Robert O'Brien reported in his San Francisco Chronicle column on Oct. 13.*

O'Brien quoted Capt Thomas E. Crowley, an officer with the 442d in Italy and France.

According to the story told by Capt Crowley to O'Brien:

"This rather fantastic action took place about a month after the 442d participated in the heroic rescue of the Lost Battalion

in the Vosges Forest. Its numbers depleted by 2100 casualties suffered in that action, the unit was shifted to the Maritime Alps between France and Italy to rest.

"One day a Nisei on lookout in a mountain observation post saw a Nazi submarine rise to the surface in a small bay. It was apparently having engine trouble. He notified headquarters, which sent down a group of men armed with 50 caliber machine guns and trench mortars. They then proceeded to attack, and after 15 minutes of fire the Nazis decided to beach the ship."

"The Nisei promptly captured the crew and packed them off in trucks to an Allied fleet base 20 miles away. They had the sub towed to the base in a tugboat. And they turned both prisoners and submarine over to the Navy without a word of explanation."

"Crowley believes the Navy may still be wondering where the hell an infantry outfit ever picked up a German U-Boat."

PACIFIC CITIZEN

2d got the high ground, the cold, ski-resort slopes of Peira Cava in the frosty Alps. The regiment guarded an 18-mile front stretching from the warm, balmy Riviera sector by the sea to the wintry cold mountains on the French-Italian border. They would hold this stationary front for the next four months.

The Combat Team was now attached to the 44th Anti-Aircraft Artillery Brigade whose mission was to guard against a possible thrust from the Franco-Italian border toward Marseille. Only the Combat Team stood between the Germans at the border and Marseille to the west. To prevent a surprise attack by the enemy and to keep them, in turn, worried about a possible attack by the Allies, frequent patrols, hit-and-run skirmishes, and minelaying parties were conducted. Even a "naval" battle was undertaken in which a two-man submarine was captured. Intermittent fire was laid down by the artillery on both sides of the border — almost, but not quite, a polite holding action. Men still got killed or wounded, medics still had to minister to the wounded, and pack-mule supply teams still had to plod their way up perilous paths to and from the lonely mountain outposts. The Champagne Campaign ofttimes belied its name.

Left, A Company outpost on the French/Italian border near Sospel, France. Above, F Company patrol on security check. Below, taking "ten" after an all-night patrol

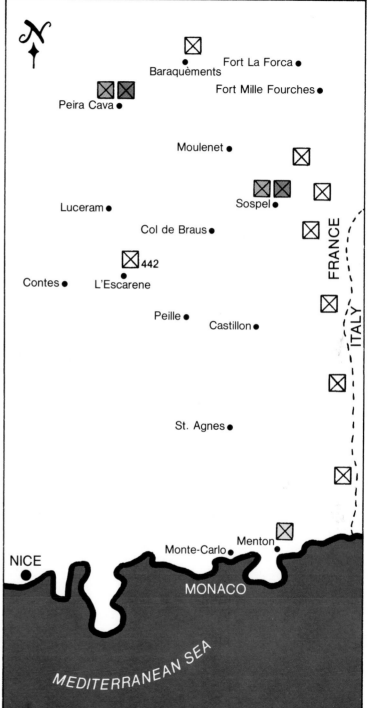

Peira Cava ●

Baraquèments ●

Fort La Forca ●

Fort Mille Fourches ●

Moulenet ●

Luceram ●

Sospel ●

Col de Braus ●

442

Contes ●　L'Escarene ●

Peille ●

Castillon ●

FRANCE

ITALY

St. Agnes ●

100th Battalion

2d Battalion

3d Battalion

Menton ●

Monte-Carlo ●

NICE ●

MONACO

MEDITERRANEAN SEA

Meanwhile, Back at the Queen's Bar in Nice

Numerous passes were issued to the men of the 100/442 even as they manned the outposts and patrolled the mountains along the Franco-Italian border. Replacements, supplies, and winter uniforms now began to arrive with regularity. The need for heavy winter clothing was most urgent in the fighting in the Vosges where the weather was cold and there was an abundance of ice and snow. According to the quartermasters, it takes a little longer to fill requisitions for a Combat Team whose average height is 5'4". Wearing heavy winter uniforms with pants too long or cuffs to the fingertips, the men headed for the sunny beaches and beguiling climes of the Riviera whenever they could wangle a pass.

They headed for Antibes, Cannes or Nice — even off-limits Monaco with its casino and gaming tables. Off

Top left, F Company, 2d Platoon, with arms, Antibes, France. Note chow line, right rear. Bottom, far left, Monte Fujita preparing "kau kau" (Hawaiian, food) at Observation Post No. 3, French/Italian border. Left, the Red Cross donut, dearly loved in Italy and France. Above, mule turns away from a load of K rations. Alps, France/Italy

clear that diet—bean power or rice power—had very little to do with "Going for Broke" or picking up a Purple Heart. A few of the many courageous officers are listed below. (We are sorry we could not list them all.)

Capt George H. Grandstaff, HQ Company, earned a Purple Heart with three Oak Leaf Clusters in addition to the Silver Star and the Legion of Merit. Capt Walter F. Johnson received the Silver Star, the Bronze Star, the Presidential Unit Citation, and the Purple Heart with an Oak Leaf Cluster. Capt Edward J. Nilges, KIA, was awarded the Silver Star, the Purple Heart, and the Presidential Unit Citation. 1st Lt Dan E. Rowlands was awarded a Silver Star, a Bronze Star and a Purple Heart with an Oak Leaf Cluster. 1st Lt Horace F. Smith, K Company platoon leader, earned a Silver Star, a Bronze Star with Oak Leaf Cluster, and a Purple Heart with Oak Leaf Cluster. 1st Lt James Wheatley, KIA, was awarded the Silver Star, the Purple Heart with three Oak Leaf Clusters, and the Presidential Unit Citation. 2d Lt Edward T. Davis led his platoon with a Silver Star, a Bronze Star, and a Purple Heart. Col Charles W. Pence received the Purple Heart, the Croix de Guerre and the Distinguished Service Medal, the only one awarded to the 100/442. Col Virgil R. Miller received the Silver Star, the Legion of Merit, the Bronze Star, and the Medaglia al Valore Militare (Italy). Lt Col James M. Hanley was awarded the Legion of Merit, the Bronze Star, and the Croix de Guerre (French). Lt Col Alfred A. Pursall earned the Silver Star, the Bronze Star, and the Croix de Guerre. Lt Col Gordon Singles was awarded the Bronze Star, the Presidential Unit Citation, and the Croix de Guerre.

● On why the 100th Infantry Battalion got the choice, balmy Riviera post while the 2d and 3d battalions got the icy alpine sectors during the "Champagne Campaign." "The 100th is the one that did the fighting, took all the objectives at Belvedere and Sassetta, did everything until we could get on our feet; we owe a debt of gratitude to the 100th . . . and I'm paying it now. What little I can. The 100th has the Riviera and the 100th is going to stay on the Riviera as long as we're here." COL CHARLES W. PENCE

● They were known as Haoles or "beanies," they were Caucasian and eschewed rice but ate it when they had to (daily). It was quite

● Sgt Masa Sakamoto was from Northern California. He was killed in Sospel. I was told to go up and get his body and bring it down. We had a little service in the cave there and it was my duty as the Chaplain to search his pockets in order to get everything home that can be sent home. I found a letter . . . all of his brothers were in the army in Japan . . . some vandals in California had burned down his father's home and barn in the name of patriotism. And yet this young man had volunteered for every patrol that he could go on. You know, you can't give a medal high enough for a man like that. We don't realize how much these boys in California had to go through . . . to find a letter like that and his going out on a patrol and being killed.

duty, they found wine, women and song — the latter, courtesy of the Combat Team's own 206th U.S. Army Ground Forces "big band." As all good things must, the band finally had to pack up its instruments (the band members served as litter bearers when the Combat Team went into action) and, with the 100/442, move on to an assembly area at Antibes. From there, they left for Marseille and their 22 March 1945 embarcation. Destination: Livorno, Italy.

Col Charles W. Pence, suffering from back wounds incurred during the Vosges action, was transferred to other duties and Col Virgil R. Miller assumed command. (Col Pence was later promoted to Brigadier General.) Lt Col James M. Hanley, 2d Battalion commander, was named Regimental Executive Officer. Maj Robert A. Gopel took command of the 2d Battalion. Maj Jack E. Conley was named Commanding Officer of the 100th Infantry Battalion.

Left, left to right — PFC Lloyd Onoye, T/Sgt Chet Tanaka, Madelyn (daughter of Monaco croupier, kneeling), S/Sgt Mitch Miyamoto, PFC William Otani, and friend (unidentified). Peille, France, December '44. Above, front row, left to right — Sgt Sanji Kimoto, T/Sgt Kazuo Asazawa, PFC James Okamoto; back row, PFC Nizae Yashima, an unidentified squad member, S/Sgt Tokuo Kajiwara, S/Sgt Tom Yamashita, and Ted Wada. All from Company K, in the French/Italian alps during the Champagne Campaign

● *Tsugimi Masuda, a Hawaiian buddhahead, and Sam Goto, a mainland kotonk, set out to relieve two other Fox Company men at an outpost on the French/Italian border. Soon after starting out, Masuda turned to Goto and said in pidgin, "I have to go back and pick up something, so you go stay go, I go stay come." Goto looked at Masuda in complete bewilderment -- he didn't know whether to go or stay. Masuda took one look at Goto's expression and broke out laughing. He realized an explanation was in order. "Sam, you keep going, I'll catch up with you later."*

522d Field Artillery Moves to Central European Theater

Near the end of the Champagne Campaign, the 522d Field Artillery Battalion was re-assigned to the 7th Army and moved back up the Rhine Valley. They joined the 63d Division from 12 March to 21 March in an assault on the Siegfried Line between central France and Germany.

The 522d was then shifted to provide supporting fire to the 45th Division when it crossed the Rhine.

Several days later, the 522d moved across the Rhine River with the 44th Division and provided supporting fire in the attack on Mannheim. When Mannheim fell, the 522d returned to the 63d Division for the Neckar River crossing and contributed to the fall of Heidelberg.

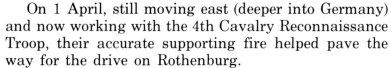

On 1 April, still moving east (deeper into Germany) and now working with the 4th Cavalry Reconnaissance Troop, their accurate supporting fire helped pave the way for the drive on Rothenburg.

There followed a stint with the 101st Airborne. The 522d had so many attachments it was gaining notoriety.

On 26 April, the 522d joined the 4th Infantry Division and crossed the Danube to take the town of Morlbach.

From the 27th to the 30th of April, the 522d fought with the 4th Division in the drive for Salzburg, Austria. Later, they supported the 101st Airborne Division in

Far left, 522d men truck to new gun positions. The 522 gave artillery support to seven divisions in Central Europe during the last month of the war. Their fire was so accurate, they were known as "the sharpshooters." Fanning out in support of the various divisions, the 522 overran many installations of the rapidly retreating enemy . . . grounded aircraft is a Heinkel 177, heavy bomber. Below the bomber is a Jagdtiger Tank mounting 128mm gun minus rear turret. At right of aircraft is a 522d supply truck sporting a Nazi eagle hood ornament. Left, Cpl John Nishimura and 2d Lt Susumu Ito, Forward Observers with I, K, and L companies during Vosges, smile as war draws to a close. Below, a bag of prisoners. Bottom right, the 3d Reich's Jagdpanzer Mark IV in mild disarray

115

their sweep of southern Germany.

To say the least, the 522d joined the Army and saw the world. In doing so, they fired over 150,000 rounds in support of seven different army divisions and units in a month and a half and achieved every objective assigned.

From May 2 to November 1945, when the 522d Field Artillery Battalion finally returned to the United States, they set up roadblocks and serviced sentry posts near Donauworth, Austria, to apprehend fleeing Nazis. They later became part of the occupation army of Austria.

The 100/442 captured a submarine, look what the 522 got! A Messerschmitt ME 262 Jet Fighter

The 522d Opens the Gate to Dachau

● *Two liaison scouts from the 522d Field Artillery Bn, 100/442 RCT, were among the first Allied troops to release prisoners in the Dachau concentration camp. I watched as one of the scouts used his carbine to shoot off the chain that held the prison gates shut. He said he just had to open the gates when he saw a couple of the 50 or so prisoners, sprawled on the snow-covered ground, moving weakly,. They weren't dead as he had first thought.*

When the gates swung open, we got our first good look at the prisoners. Many of them were Jews. They were wearing black and white striped prison suits and round caps. A few had shredded blanket rags draped over their shoulders. It was cold and the snow was two feet deep in some places. There were no German guards. They had taken off before we reached the camp.

The prisoners struggled to their feet after the gates were opened. They shuffled weakly out of the compound. They were like skeletons — all skin and bones.

Outside the compound, there were a couple of dead cows lying on the road. In minutes, the prisoners had cut off strips of meat, roasted them over a small fire and were gobbling the food down. They were starving. After they finished eating, they moved on down the road and took shelter in a large stable. They insisted on staying in the stable and refused to spend another night in Dachau.

We had been ordered not to give out rations to the Dachau prisoners because the war was still on and such supplies were needed to keep our own fighting strength up, but we gave them food, clothing and medical supplies anyway. The officers looked the other way. These prisoners really needed help and they needed it right away. They were sick, starving and dying.

I saw one GI throw some orange peelings into a garbage can. One of the prisoners grabbed the peelings, tore them into small pieces and shared them with the others. They hadn't had any fruit or vegetables in months. They had scurvy. Their teeth were falling out of their gums.

We stayed near Dachau for several days and then got orders to move on. During this time, I found some large chalk-like bars, sort of oval-shaped, with numbers stamped on them. I was about to "liberate" a couple of them as souvenirs when an MP told me they were the remains of prisoners. The numbers were for identification. I put the bars back.

FROM THE DIARY OF
T/4 ICHIRO IMAMURA
MEDICAL DETACHMENT
522d FIELD ARTILLERY BATTALION

100/442 leaving Marseille, France, for Italy, March 1945. Note truck loaded with duffle bags. Troops closed into Peninsula Base Section Staging Area then left by truck for Pietrasanta and Valle-chio, moving into assault position by hiking all night up narrow mountain paths

The Po Valley Campaign

The 100th and the 442d closed into the Peninsula Base Section Staging Area at Pisa on 25 March 1945 and were assigned to the 5th Army, attached to the IV Corps, and under the operational control of the 92d Infantry Division. The arrival of the 100/442 was kept a closely guarded secret from the Germans. Gen Mark Clark had ordered the return of the Combat Team for a critical mission — spearhead a diversionary assault on the western sector of the Gothic Line.

For nine months, Field Marshall Kesselring directed the construction of fortifications in the rugged mountains of the Apennines. They were built under the direction of the infamous, slave-labor Todt organization. Approximately 15,000 Italians were forced to dig or blast anti-tank ditches, gun emplacements, machine-gun nests, rifle pits, and trenches. The Germans were entrenched in positions drilled out of solid rock and reinforced with concrete. A string of these rock fortifications ran from the coastal area to the mountains of Carchio and Altissimo and beyond. These fortress-like machine-gun nests — 2,376 along the entire Gothic Line — produced interlocking fire; other OP's (observation posts) commanded an unparallelled view of the valleys. Cut into the mountaintops, they were a double-barreled threat that dominated the terrain for miles. During the months prior to the arrival of the 100/442, Allied planes had bombed the positions, strafed them, and zeroed-in artillery fire — to no avail. The Germans were basking in an impregnable stronghold.

The hill mass, west to east, was known as Georgia, Florida, Ohio 1, 2 and 3, Mount Cerreta, Mount Folgorita, Mount Carchio, and Mount Altissimo. Mount Altissimo, over 3,000 feet tall, towered over the other mountains. It had an OP carved into solid rock at its military crest, which was able to spot practically everything that moved in the valley below. Even the sighting of a single GI would draw a round of mortar fire.

One more shot before going into line, Gothic, that is. Standing, left to right: PFC Jimmy Nakamura, PFC Conrad Kuruhara, PFC Takami Misaki, PFC Satoshi Kaneshiro, Sgt Toshio Funai, T/Sgt Albert Takahashi, S/Sgt Haru Fujii, 1st Sgt Yeiki Matsui, PFC Paul Nishimoto, S/Sgt Akira Watanabe, S/Sgt Tom Matsumoto, PFC Kenneth Nakano

How to Attack a Mountain Fortress

Carefully.

After much consultation, the Regimental Commander, Col Virgil R. Miller, and 3d Battalion Commander, Lt Col Alfred A. Pursall, narrowed their attack plans to three sets of alternatives: (1) frontal or pincers; (2) daylight or night; and (3) conventional or surprise. The combination of frontal, daylight, conventional attack had been tried before with no success. It was decided to try a pincers attack at dawn with the surprise element of an all-night climb to get in position for the dawn assault.

This plan would require the climbing of a sheer 3,000-foot mountain face in the dark with full fighting gear. It would have to be done in absolute silence without voice or radio communication to maintain the element of surprise.

On 3 April, the 100th Battalion moved into a forward assembly area in the vicinity of Vallechio and remained in concealment. That same night, the 3d Battalion detrucked at Pietrasanta and climbed eight tortuous miles in the dark, up mountain trails to Azzano, a mountain village that was under enemy observation during the daylight hours. The unit also remained under cover until the next night. It then moved out to descend into the valley and then moved on to scale the 3,000-foot saddle between Mount Cerreta and Mount Folgorita.

To prepare for the night climb, the men smudged their hands and faces with soot and dirt, taped their dog tags (metal identification plates) to keep them from rattling, and placed a complete ban on lights, radio and just plain talking.

On the night of 4 April, companies I, L and M of the 3d Battalion moved down the steep valley facing Azzano and up to the saddle. It was an eight-hour climb up an almost vertical, shale-covered mountainside. It was grasping in the dark for a few, shallow-rooted shrubs, or your buddy's rifle butt, or his boot. When several of the men fell with full field packs, rifle and ammo, there was no crying out in spite of injuries. The men made it to the top. They did not break the silence.

That same night, still maintaining absolute silence, the 100th went into line on Florida Hill, relieving elements of the 371st Infantry. The 100th was now poised for the attack against Georgia and Ohio 1, 2 and 3. The Anti-Tank Company was split up for special duty as carrying parties and litter bearers. One platoon was assigned to the 100th, one platoon to the 2d Battalion, and two platoons to the 3d Battalion.

Left, village of Azzano in foreground faces 3,000-foot Mount Folgorita. I, L, and M companies made the eight-hour all-night climb to get into attack position at dawn, 5 April 1945. Above, mortar crew in position to support attacking riflemen

FLA.   Georgia

This photo, taken one month before the 100/442 attack, was handmarked by Army Intelligence to indicate Florida and Georgia hills. Redoubts in the hills had been fortified and strengthened by the enemy for six months. The 100/442 overran them in 32 minutes

At dawn 0500, 5 April 1945, the men were in position; the pincers were set for the surprise attack against the enemy. The 100th attacked frontally against Georgia after a tremendous barrage of artillery fire from the joined batteries of the 599th and 229th Artillery Battalions, the 442d Regimental Cannon Company, Company B of the 895th Tank Destroyer Battalion, Company B of the 84th Chemical Battalion (4.2 mortars), and the Assault Gun Platoon of the 758th Tank Battalion.

After the first several hundred yards of advance, eight mines blew up. Entrenched machine-guns opened fire and grenades rained down on the men of the 100th. The drive faltered. PFC Henry Y. Arao (later S/Sgt) of A Company gave first aid to his wounded squad leader, reorganized the squad and led them forward against the machine-gun nest. He went on alone, crawling through a thick minefield, and tossed a grenade into the nest. Then he machine-gunned the first gunner and took the second gunner prisoner. When another machine gun opened up, PFC Arao again advanced alone, threw another grenade, killed the gunners and sent the support enemy infantry scurrying in retreat. This heroic feat earned PFC Henry Y. Arao the Distinguished Service Cross.

In the same battle, PFC Sadao S. Munemori, an assistant squad leader of A Company, took charge when his squad leader was wounded. PFC Munemori made a frontal, one-man attack on two machine-gun nests and knocked both out with hand grenades. Withdrawing under murderous fire and a shower of enemy grenades, he had nearly reached the safety of a shell hole when an unexploded grenade bounced off his helmet and tumbled toward two of his comrades. Rising up amidst the withering small arms fire, he dove on top of the live grenade and smothered the blast with his body. He was killed, but his comrades were spared. PFC Sadao S. Munemori was awarded the Congressional Medal of Honor for this heroic action beyond the call of duty.

By 0532, the men of the 100th had secured the military crest of Georgia Hill. The pincers were working; the surprise attack had succeeded. In 32 minutes, the 100/442 had smashed a redoubt that had withstood Allied assaults for over five months. This did not mean the enemy was totally defeated; many strong-points yet remained. Artillery and mortar fire continued to fall on

Medal of Honor

PFC Sadao S. Munemori was awarded the Medal of Honor, posthumously, 13 March 1946

THE MEDAL OF HONOR

"For extraordinary heroism above and beyond the call of duty"

PFC Sadao S. Munemori left the Military Intelligence Service to volunteer for combat duty with the 100/442. He joined Company A of the 100th Infantry Battalion at Anzio on May 8, 1944 and earned his Combat Infantryman Badge before the day was out. Within a year, PFC Munemori was awarded the highest decoration that the Army could give, the Congressional Medal of Honor.

April 5, 1945 was the kick-off date for the 100/442 drive against the "impregnable" Gothic Line. Their objective: Georgia Hill, nestling among Florida and Ohio 1, 2 and 3 hill masses near the western coastal plains of Pietrasanta.

After a predawn, ten-minute barrage of the enemy positions, Company A charged into the area. They were met by a hail of machine-gun fire and grenade bursts. The Squad Leader of the forward unit was wounded. PFC Munemori took over and led his men through a minefield, advancing to within 30 yards of a strongly entrenched machine-gun nest. Heavy fire forced the men to take cover in the shallow shell craters blasted out by the early morning barrage. Grabbing a half dozen grenades, PFC Munemori made a frontal, one-man attack through heavy fire until he was about 15 yards away from the machine gun nest. Then he lobbed in grenade after grenade until he knocked out both machine guns and wounded two of the German gunners. PFC Munemori then worked his way back toward his squad, followed by bursting grenades. As he neared the crater where his men were waiting, a grenade bounced off his helmet and rolled into the crater. Without hesitation, PFC Munemori dove on the grenade and smothered the explosion with his body. He was killed instantly. His two squad members escaped with their lives. PFC Akira Shishido suffered a concussion. Pvt Jimi Oda received a fragment in the eye. The platoon was then joined by another platoon and drove the Germans from their strongly defended positions.

By his swift, supremely heroic action, PFC Munemori saved the lives of two of his men at the cost of his own. He also did much to clear the path for his company's later victorious advance.

A Congressional Medal of Honor commemorating PFC Munemori's heroism was presented to his mother, Mrs. Nawa Munemori, on March 13, 1946.

Later, a tanker was renamed in his honor. The "Sadao S. Munemori" became the first U.S. military ship to bear a Japanese name.

Above, "the other side of the mountain" — the 100th takes Ohio 1, 2, and 3 hills. This is what it looks like? Right bottom, S/Sgt Harry H.

Hamada, Company K, displaying enemy materiel, "What they don't have, they can't use and that's got to be good"

Ohio 1, 2 and 3 as the 100th pressed on. The enemy counterattacked that night, but the 100th held.

On the right flank, the 3d Battalion jumped off from the top of the saddle after their all-night climb. This time, the enemy was caught completely by surprise. By 0600, the attack was in full force. L Company moved south along the saddle ridge toward Mount Folgorita while I Company dispatched one platoon north along a spur toward Mount Carchio.

The Germans called on their coastal and railroad guns at Punta Bianca, La Spezia, for assistance, but L Company in an act of sheer, raw courage determinedly moved through the artillery and mortar fire and took on the defenders in hand-to-hand combat. They killed six of the enemy, captured four, and sent the rest fleeing down the west side of Mount Folgorita.

K Company and a mortar platoon of M Company left Azzano and tried to climb Mount Folgorita in daylight. Enemy observers on Mount Altissimo called down accurate mortar fire, killing 17, and wounding 83. At the end of the day, the Germans suffered 30 dead, 5 wounded or captured, 12 bunkers destroyed and the loss of 17 machine guns and 3 '75mm' mountain howitzers, as well as several tons of ammunition and supplies.

In this one day of battle, the Gothic Line was cracked. This crack would soon widen into a full-size fracture.

The next day, 6 April, the pincers closed even tighter. The ridge-line from Florida to Folgorita had been taken. F Company was pulled off to assist I Company in mopping up elements of enemy resistance on Mount Carchio. Ohio 1, 2 and 3 was still being stubbornly held by the Germans but was reduced by the end of the day through a classic cooperation of fire from air, artillery, and infantry. The last ridge link, Mount Cerreta, finally fell to a determined assault by L Company of the 3d Battalion. L Company lost 2 men killed and 11 men wounded in this action; the enemy, 20 men killed and 11 men captured.

• *T/4 Eji Suyama, a member of Lt Col Pursall's Executive Command Group, moving abreast with the attacking rifle companies, knocked out a machine-gun nest on the military crest of the reverse slope of Mount Folgorita with two shots slowly squeezed out of his M-1. It was a classic example of "how to fire an M-1." Shot one knocked out gunner number one. Shot two knocked out gunner number two. No ammo wasted. Two shots, two down. One less machine-gun nest. T/4 Suyama received a Silver Star for this exploit.*

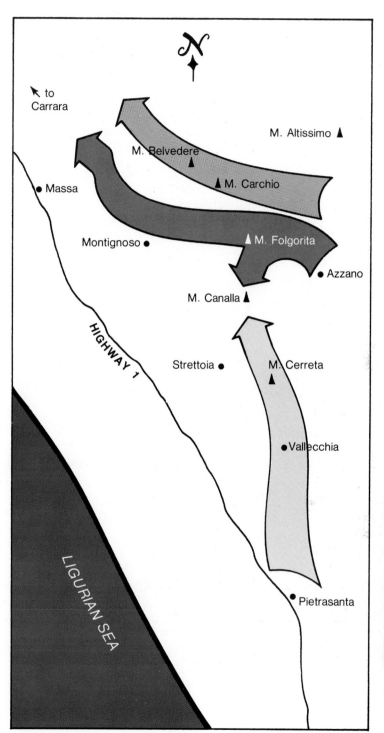

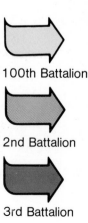
100th Battalion

2nd Battalion

3rd Battalion

Machine Gun Battalion Kesselring

Mount Belvedere was a German stronghold held by the crack Machine Gun Battalion Kesselring. The 2d Battalion had climbed Mount Folgorita the previous night to get into position, running into vicious mortar fire and thunderous blasting from the coastal guns of Punta Bianca. Now the veteran Kesselring troops gave ground grudgingly against the determined attack of the 2d Battalion.

It was here at Mount Belvedere that T/Sgt Yukio Okutsu of F Company knocked out three machine-gun nests. Held up by a trio of machine-guns, T/Sgt Okutsu crawled 30 yards to the first emplacement and threw in two grenades to wipe out the gunners. Running from cover to cover, he hit the second machine-gun emplacement with a grenade, wounding two and capturing two. He was momentarily stunned by a ricocheting bullet but charged the third machine-gun nest with his Tommy gun, capturing the four-man crew. For this courageous action, T/Sgt Okutsu received the Distinguished Service Cross.

After two days of bitter fighting, Mount Belvedere finally fell to the 2d Battalion. The Germans lost 106 men as prisoners and the Kesselring Machine Gun Battalion was almost, as the Germans might say, *kaput.*

Mopping Up Operations

The 7th was primarily a day of cleaning and mopping up. The 100th and the 3d Battalion each cleared the Germans out of their areas. Company K overshot its mark and circled behind the enemy to capture 20 Germans, four 81mm mortars, and a large supply of ammo. The 2d Battalion finished securing the peak on Mount Belvedere.

On 8 April, the 3d Battalion moved along the Colle Piano ridge and secured the village of Montignoso. Highway 1 to Massa was now open, and supplies and replacements that formerly took a day to reach the Combat Team could now be brought up in a few hours.

The 2d Battalion led by G Company ran into enemy

Above, moment of truth — get the grenade off before he gets you.
Right, down from the mountains, into the towns, then right back up

opposition along the Colle Tecchione spur. G Company waged a fierce battle all afternoon against two enemy companies. They encountered artillery, mortar, and automatic fire. By nightfall, G Company had taken 6 prisoners, killed 8, and seized 3 machine guns and 4 mortars. The Germans counterattacked at midnight, but they were beaten back. The next day, the fight continued. M and K Companies joined in the fray. M Company pounded the enemy positions with mortars for three hours. This drove the enemy into the open, where they were hit by artillery. Company K captured 50 Germans along with 4 mortars and 7 machine guns.

The other two companies of the 2d Battalion, E and F, attacked the towns of Altagnana and Pariana. E Company took Altagnana with only slight opposition. Pariana was another story. Here were the final remnants of the once-invincible Machine-Gun Battalion Kesselring. The Germans drove off an F Company patrol that night. The next day and night saw bitter fighting between a combined platoon of F Company and H Company against 150 Kesselring veterans. By nightfall, Pariana was taken. In this action, 65 Germans were killed, 62 prisoners were taken and 12 mortars and 8 machine guns were liberated. Machine Gun Battalion Kesselring was officially *kaput!*

● *When a prisoner was captured, and there would be several, we put one outside the door and we'd bring the other one in. I would start questioning the one inside the room loudly in German, my best familiar German, and if they didn't answer I would have him taken out another door, other than the door he came in. The waiting German prisoner could hear me screaming, "Take him out and shoot him." Course we wouldn't shoot him. But they would take him out the other door and shoot a rifle in the air. And then I would say, "Bring in the next one." Usually he would talk, a lot better than the first one.*

On to Carrara

On the 10th, the 100/442 continued their attack. The Germans had pulled back beyond Carrara but their massive coastal guns from Punta Bianca continued to rake Massa and Highway 1 leading into it. The 473d Infantry had taken Massa with slight opposition. The 100/442 bypassed Massa, moved 3,000 yards beyond the Frigido River and secured the high ground overlooking Carrara, the great marble-quarrying center of Italy. The 3d Battalion was now in the foothills, the 2d Battalion was on 3,000-foot Mount Brugiana which dominated the area, and the 100th was again on guard on the right flank near Antona. The Anti-Tank Company was to block the roads leading into Massa from the east.

On 11 April, L Company moved down into Carrara and found the town occupied by the Partisans. K Company bypassed Carrara and pushed north into the moun-

They may be retreating, but they're still shooting. GI's scramble for cover through doorway as enemy artillery comes in. Right, Maj Claude White directs traffic at Montignoso supply dump. Far right, convoy stops for "ten-minute break" in shelter of cliff

tains, taking Gragnana and Sorgnano without opposition. On the right flank, the 100th trudged eight miles over the mountains and seized Colonnata to secure the right flank abreast.

The 100/442 Regimental Combat Team was moving so fast they had almost outdistanced their supply line. The 232d Combat Engineers were still busy clearing Highway 1 between Massa and Carrara. They had run into a mess of mines and high-explosive boobytraps; three 'dozers were blown up and the constant sniper fire didn't help. But by the 12th, they had cleared the way and supplies rolled into Carrara from Massa.

The 13th was not the luckiest day of the Po Valley Campaign. The 2d Battalion had moved five miles north of Carrara, passing Gragnana and Castelpoggio without opposition. Then they pressed their luck too far. They moved onto the base of Mount Pizzacuto, and the Germans opened up. The German OP on the mountain could see every move of the 2d Battalion as well as the 100th a mile and a half behind the 2d. Our artillery could not keep pace with them, but the German artillery could. The enemy's self-propelleds pinned down both the 2d Battalion and the 100th. The 3d Battalion, in reserve in Carrara, also took a pounding from the coastal batteries at La Spezia and Punta Bianca. All in all, it was a bad day, and noisy.

But that night the situation started to improve. First, Allied artillery finally caught up with the 2d and the 100th. Then Company B was sent under cover of darkness to Castelpoggio to support the 2d Battalion command group. Unfortunately for the Germans, they did not know about these new developments. At dawn, the

Above, yet another Italian village surrounded by blasted and broken trees, low rock-rubble fences, and knee-high drainage ditches. Where is the enemy? We spread out and move forward. Right: the enemy opens up—we hit the ground fast. He's got a

enemy attacked Castelpoggio in battalion strength. Company B, with an assist from Company H's heavy weapons, blocked the attack. The enemy suffered 16 KIA, 8 WIA. B and H Companies had 5 dead and 5 wounded.

G Company, with the artillery and mortar support now at their disposal, called for fire and blasted the enemy positions on Mount Pizzacuto. By noon, they took the mountain and chased the enemy down the hill and up the next hill to Fort Bastione. By nightfall, G Company had killed 16 Germans and taken 54 prisoners.

Company F had secured Mount Pizzacuto while Company G had moved out to prepare for the assault on Fort Bastione for the following day.

On 15 April, following a heavy bomb and artillery attack on Fort Bastione, Company G attacked and, by 1300, had taken the Fort. Elements of Company G continued on with F Company to attack the next objective, Mount Grugola. Opposition was light, and the hilltop was secured by the 2d Battalion in a matter of hours.

In the meantime, fierce fighting raged on La Bandita Ridge, west of Castelpoggio. Company C and the 232d

machine gun in the blown-out house ahead and another behind a rock wall for crossfire. Sometimes he backs up his play with mortar or artillery fire. One squad moves forward. The others give covering fire. Some make it. Some don't.

Combat Engineers met a strong German counterattack and fought from mid-afternoon till dark. M Company dumped over 400 rounds of mortars on the German positions, forcing the enemy to withdraw. Company C had 10 men WIA. The Engineers' commander, Capt Pershing Nakada, was also wounded in action.

While Company C was mopping up at La Bandita, Company B moved through Fort Bastione and attacked southwest down the ridge to clear that area. The 3d Battalion had moved out of Carrara to relieve the 2d Battalion. K Company went up and down Mount Pizzacuto to seize Mount Tomaggiora after a brief firefight.

● *I was hit in Italy. We were walking through the dry stream bed. I had just about made the turn on a bend when they started shelling. I didn't realize I got hit. I couldn't walk, you see, and rocks were flying all around. I had blood all over my face. So I limped and stayed there as a liaison. I told the incoming troops, "Don't go this way." I started directing them. I'd say, "Go the other way, go the other way because the bend is under fire." That's where the shells were coming in. So I stood there and told them to go the other way, go the other way. The boys that saw me, thought I got hit all over my face. It wasn't so. It was just blood dripping from the stones that flew, you know, and the shrapnel was in my right thigh.*

A Hornets' Nest

On 17 April, other elements of the 3d Battalion tried to take the town of Fosdinova and Mount Nebbione. They ran into an angry hornets' nest. The Germans were determined to hold these strategic points at all cost because they controlled the terrain around the vital road center of Aulla. If the enemy lost Aulla, La Spezia on the coast would be cut off. Genoa to the north was now in the hands of the Partisans. The only way out for the German coastal troops was through Aulla, and both sides knew it!

Then the Germans blew up their railroad guns at Punta Bianca, La Spezia. They were making ready to run for Aulla before it fell — they blew their fortifications and left for points northeast, through the Po Valley. The fighting at this point became quite intense.

Company E's 1st Lt Daniel Inouye, now Senator from Hawaii, led one of the attacking units against the determined and entrenched enemy troops. In spite of serious wounds, he single-handedly destroyed two machine-gun nests. His right arm was all but blown away by a rifle grenade and he had been shot in the stomach; the blasts had knocked him down twice, but still he refused to stay down. He kept rising to his feet to throw grenades, to shoot his Tommy gun with his left hand, and to direct his men. The third volley of fire hit him in the thigh, and sent him rolling down the hill. Unbelievably, when his men reached his side, he warned them where enemy fire was coming from! Lt Inouye received the Distinguished Service Cross for this action.

Mt. Nebbione and the surrounding hills were the last piece of high ground before Aulla. The Germans had to hold these ridges to ensure an escape route from the coastal area of La Spezia. On the 19th, the 2d and the 3d Battalions assaulted Mt. Nebbione but the enemy held. The

---

● *"Clearing a hill" or "capturing prisoners" may sound like a routine, work-a-day operation — "a piece of cake." It wasn't. It could be like any other combat day, and any other day in combat is a day with tension so tight you leave your fingerprints on your rifle butt. You listen unconsciously to the small arms or machine-gun fire and note immediately by the sound whether it is theirs or ours. You scan every bush and shrub and ravine from 50 to 500 yards for any unusual movement, a glint of metal or glass against the sunlight. You try to blot out the thought that your next step might be on a Schuh mine — all wood, it cannot be picked up by a mine detector — or against a trip wire. You move forward at a half crouch. Everything is a blur yet you note where your buddies are. It is so quiet but you know all hell could break loose now, at any minute, or tomorrow. You never know when, but you have to be up and ready.*

Some men could sustain this pitch for days and weeks; others could not. It was not something to be ashamed of if you broke under the stress. It was natural. Different men had different breaking points. So when you read, "they cleared hill such and such," or "finished off" the enemy, it really was not that simple. It was different men, fighting and undergoing combat stress or fatigue to varying degrees. When you "cleared" an area or "took some prisoners" you could be calm and collected or you could be "trigger happy." People could get killed needlessly. But no combat soldier would fault another if he shot too fast or dropped one too many grenades. War is not that neat. It was definitely not "a piece of cake."

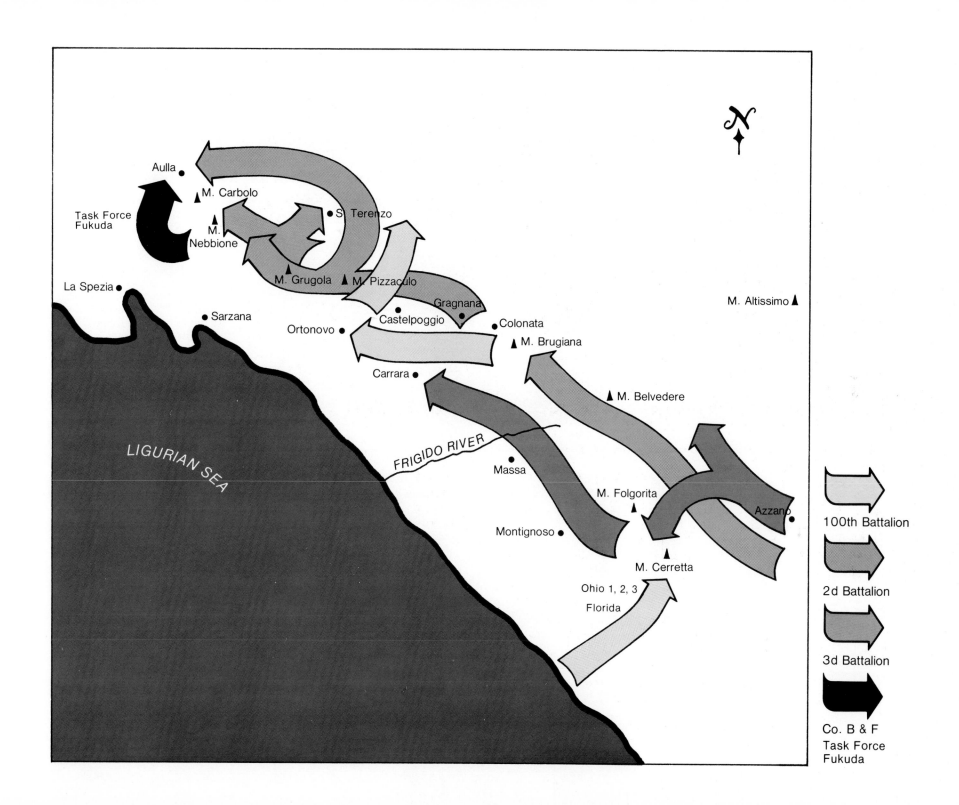

Task Force Fukuda

LIGURIAN SEA

Aulla

M. Carbolo

S. Terenzo

M. Nebbione

M. Grugola M. Pizzaculo

La Spezia

Sarzana

Gragnana

Castelpoggio Colonata

Ortonovo

M. Brugiana

Carrara

M. Altissimo

M. Belvedere

FRIGIDO RIVER

Massa

M. Folgorita

Montignoso

Azzano

M. Cerretta

Ohio 1, 2, 3

Florida

100th Battalion

2d Battalion

3d Battalion

Co. B & F
Task Force
Fukuda

• *Daniel K. Inouye volunteered for the 442d when a youngster of 19, as a private. He received a combat commission in Italy in 1944, eventually being discharged as a captain. His great moment came in the closing stage of the war in the Mediterranean, on April 20, 1945, during the final Allied drive. Inouye was leading an attack by Company E against the 3rd Battalion of the crack 361st Panzer Grenadier Regiment, dug in to defend Mount Nebbione, on the formidable Gothic Line. This was the main part of the Germans' final resistance before Genoa and the Po Valley.*

Lieutenant Inouye first led his platoon in a rapid encirclement that resulted in destruction of a German mortar observation post and brought his men to within 40 yards of the main hostile force. The enemy, dug into bunkers and rock crevices, fought back fanatically, halting the advance with crossfire from three machine guns which swept the area clear of cover and concealment. Inouye crawled up the slope to within five yards of the enemy and tossed two hand grenades into the machine gun nest. Before the enemy recovered, he stood up and raked the second gun with the fire from his tommy gun, killing the crew. He was hit once, but he continued to fire at the other emplacements until his arm was shattered by a grenade. In spite of his pain and his wound, he refused evacuation and directed the final assault which carried the ridge. In the attack, 25 Germans were killed and 8 others captured. For this action, Inouye received the Distinguished Service Cross. He also earned the Bronze Star Medal, the Purple Heart with two Oak Leaf Clusters, five battle stars (campaigns), the Combat Infantryman's Badge, and the Presidential Distinguished Unit Citation with four Oak Leaf Clusters.

CONGRESSMAN LIONEL VAN DEERLIN

100th took their objectives, the towns of Marciaso and Posterla as well as a hill overlooking Viano.

On April 22 in the 3d Battalion sector at Tendola, some ten miles before Aulla, Company K was held up by machine-gun fire. Pvt Joe Hayashi of Company K led his men to within 100 yards of the first machine-gun nest. Then, advancing alone, Pvt Hayashi threw a hand grenade into the nest, killing one German and forcing the other crew members to surrender. Spotting another nest of four guns, Pvt Hayashi fired a rifle grenade and knocked it out. A third nest was also decommissioned when he opened fire with his weapon and killed four of the crew. As he moved forward to continue the attack, he was shot and killed. For these heroic deeds at Tendola, Pvt Joe Hayashi was awarded the Distinguished Service Cross.

On April 23, Maj Mitsuyoshi Fukuda led a Task Force — composed of Company B, Company F, and a platoon from Anti-Tank Company — from Viano to a road junction before Aulla. This same day, the 3d Battalion seized Mt. Nebbione and Mt. Carbolo; the 2d Battalion routed the Italian Bersaghiere troops at San Terenzo, killing 40 and taking 135 prisoners.

●*DES MOINES, Ia.—The combination of Japanese American infantrymen of the 442d Regiment and Italian Partisans led by a fighting priest called Pietro, proved the winning formula in the capture of the strategic Italian coastal towns of Massa and Carrara and a lot of German prisoners in the Fifth Army's new offensive, Richard Mowrer, correspondent of the Des Moines Register, radioed in a copyrighted dispatch from the newly active Italian front last week.*

Mowrer declared that "following up their sharp thrust of the last few days along the Fifth Army's coastal flank, the Nisei Americans still were rampaging somewhere in the mountains Friday (April 13) as this correspondent went north along the shore as far as he could go."

"Every now and then," Mowrer said, "small bunches of bewildered and exhausted prisoners arrived in shell-torn Massa with reports that 'Turks' had been added to this front of many nationalities."

"The Germans think they (the Nisei) are terrible. The Partisans think they are wonderful. It's all in the point of view," Mowrer reported.

DES MOINES REGISTER

The End of the Line

On 25 April 1945, the roof caved in on the Germans.

For openers, the 2d Battalion and Task Force Fukuda drove in from the south and east to capture Aulla. With the fall of Aulla, the Combat Team pursued the rapidly retreating enemy up the Ligurian coast. They followed the fleeing troops in anything that rolled — jeeps, trucks, halftracks, whatever. Every bend in the road during the chase became a potential trap — a point where the retreating enemy might zero-in his artillery — yet not even this possibility slowed the Combat Team's pursuit.

Pvt Joe Sugawara, Cincinnati, pulling the four-legged critter known as a mule. Pvt T. Takagi, Hayden, Arizona, hangs on to the mule's tail and gets an assist up the trail

On one of the many ridges that the 100/442 had to take. Here, two of the men of the 100th await medics

● *The 232d Combat Engineer Company was just one gutsy outfit. In support of the 100/442, they built 26 by-passes, 6 culverts, 10 fills, and 4 bridges; removed over 300 mines and hundreds of booby-traps; and hauled away over a ton of dynamite from five unblown bridges. In addition, they strung over 10,000 yards of barbed wire, laid more than 50 trip flares, and seeded more than 4,200 anti-personnel mines. They also filled thousands of sandbags, built a mile of corduroy road under enemy fire, constructed mule sheds and miles of mule trails, and pulled a two-man submarine from the sea at Menton, Italy. As if all this were not enough for less than a year's work, they served as infantry riflemen in the Rome-Arno campaign, the rescue of the "Lost Battalion," and in the Po Valley campaign, as the occasion demanded. They captured over 20 prisoners and earned a Presidential Unit Citation in the process. But as far as the men of the 100/442 are concerned, their greatest exploit was the construction and maintenance of the longest running, floating mobile hot-water shower in the U.S. Army. Constructed from parts liberated from American, German, French, Swiss, and Italian plumbing and sundry industries, it was a "Rube Goldberg" affair; but the 232d Combat Engineers made it work.*

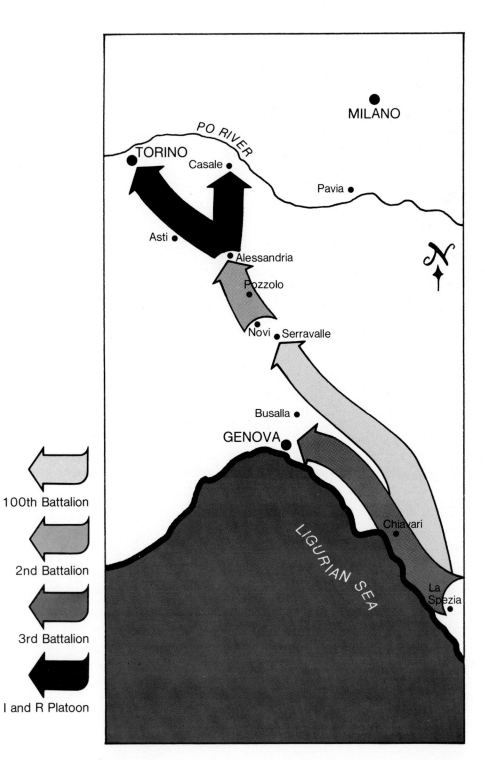

100th Battalion

2nd Battalion

3rd Battalion

I and R Platoon

- *During the shelling of Anzio and later during the Po Valley campaign near Aulla, a railroad gun that could hit a target 75 miles away was located at La Spezia. This gun was known as "Big Bertha" in World War I. In World War II it was called the "Anzio Express." This was an additional long-range artillery piece along with the huge coastal batteries at Punta Bianca in La Spezia.*

- *NEW YORK—"No soldiers we have sent abroad have a more distinguished record than these Nisei," the New York Times declared in an editorial, "Action in Italy," on April 11.*

  "On the record none surpasses them in loyalty, devotion or courage," the Times said.

  The leading New York newspaper declared that Gen Mark Clark was using "battle-tried Nisei, as Americans of Japanese ancestry call themselves" in the forefront of the 5th Army's new drive up the Ligurian coast.

  "Brought into action from rest billets in France, they have wrested from the Germans a series of towering peaks," the Times added.

  The editorial on the Japanese Americans continued:

  "More than 17,600 have been inducted into the Army. The men of the famous 100th Battalion are typical. They were originally Hawaiian volunteers but heavy losses brought replacements from many sections. Distinguished Service Crosses are commonplace. Private Jesse Hirata won his by seizing a shovel when his rifle jammed, charging an enemy nest and capturing its occupants armed with a machine-gun pistol, rifle and grenades.

  "Most of the Nisei want to fight in the Pacific. They believe that, raised in the institutions of democracy, they are better soldiers than Japanese of their own generation . . . But they do not differ in appearance from our Pacific enemy and would invite attempts at enemy infiltration. Some are used as interpreters and specialists but they have seen combat service chiefly in Italy and France. Thus far they have won every fight they have been in. But their hardest fight of all is still ahead and may outlast the war. It is the fight against prejudice roused by color of skin and slant of eye. It is easy to admire them while they are still in uniform. It would be kinder to remember and reward them when the battle is over."

PACIFIC CITIZEN
APRIL 1945

Said Hitler to Kesselring

It is reputed that Adolf Hitler told Field Marshall Kesselring, "Hold the Gothic Line at all costs." A determined 100/442 Regimental Combat Team helped to countermand these orders. The Combat Team's spearhead on the western anchor of the Gothic Line opened a crack that widened to unleash the full might of the 5th Army. A diversionary action had exploded into a full-scale attack. The Panzers and the Blitzkriegers were now in complete rout.

T/Sgt Shig Doi, I Company, 3d Bn, kneels beside pillbox, Genoa, Italy. His buddy peers out of opened steel doors. Elements of 3d Bn penetrated Genoa by riding in on streetcars!

The German anti-aircraft gun known as the Flak 36, a rapid fire 37mm weapon. Note rings on barrel — nine aircraft were downed by this enemy unit

Genoa was now in the hands of the Partisans. The 3d Battalion consolidated the control of Genoa by commandeering trolleys to convoy its troops to the center of the city. What a way to win a war. Going to work by streetcar!

The 100th took Busalla. The 2d moved on through to Alessandra and to Asti, the champagne center. There, they took 1,000 prisoners and an equal number of bottles of champagne into custody. The I & R (Intelligence and Reconnaissance) Platoon raced ahead in their halftracks to claim Turin along with the Partisans.

Even the Chaplain's corps got into the act. Chaplain Hiro Higuchi of the 2d Battalion continued merrily

Above, PFC Jimmy Nakamura, 1st Sgt Yeiki Matsui, and S/Sgt Akira Watanabe, Baker Company, enjoy the quiet before the assault on the Gothic Line, 4 April 1945. Right, PFC George Uchimiya (sunglasses) and S/Sgt Tom Takahashi display an arsenal of captured enemy weapons. Foreground, left to right, MG 34 and MG 42 machine guns with 50-round drums and 250-round belt boxes; background, left to right, gas mask cannister, spare MG 42 barrel, Mauser Kar 98k, and a Beretta MP 739 submachine gun. SS camouflage poncho serves as a backdrop

---

● *The War Department announced . . . that "members of the 442d Infantry Regiment, composed of American doughboys of Japanese descent," were "in the vanguard of the Fifth Army's great offensive which has smashed the German Army in northern Italy."*

The Japanese Americans made "sensational gains of 76 miles in five days," the War Department noted, reporting that the 442d took part in the capture of Genoa, Italy's largest seaport, on April 27, and then forged ahead to enter Turin, the last great city in the Po River valley, on April 30.

ahead of the entire battalion after he and his jeep driver did not get notice to take a "ten-minute break." By the time he got the word, he had already liberated the next town.

The Germans were completely demoralized. They were battered and at the end of the line. Their supplies had been cut off by accurate bombing of the several mountain passes which had served as their supply route. Their every step had been dogged by pursuing Allied troops and growing forces of Partisans. The German soldier was surrendering by the thousands.

By May 2, 1945, the war was over in Italy. By May 9, the war was officially over in Europe. Germany had unconditionally surrendered.

Good news — but no wild celebrations — mixed with sadness that those who went before us couldn't be with us today

M Company's 1st/Sgt Fred Dobana and T/Sgt Goro Tsuchida hold captured enemy flag with the swastika in the center

● *The 442d Regimental Combat Team . . . is cited for outstanding accomplishment in combat . . . by executing a diversionary attack on the Ligurian coast (Carrara, Italy, April 1945) . . . a daring and skillful flanking attack on the positions which formed the western anchor of the formidable Gothic line. In 4 days, the attack destroyed positions which had withstood efforts . . . for five months. The 442d drove forward despite heavy casualties . . . allowing the enemy no time for rest or reorganization . . . liberated the city of Carrara, seized the heights beyond . . . and opened the way for advances on the key road center and ports of La Spezia and Genoa . . . The successful accomplishment of this mission turned a diversionary action into a full-scale and victorious offensive . . . an important part in the final destruction of the German armies in Italy.*

GEN DWIGHT D. EISENHOWER
CHIEF OF STAFF

● *It's been over forty years, yet I see and hear these guys like it was only yesterday.*

I met Joe Shiomichi and Lloyd "Ox" Onoye in training, before we went overseas. How we got together I don't know. We were from different companies — Joe was from Easy, Ox from I, while I was from King.

Joe and I used to discuss war, politics, religion and sex — not necessarily in that order — endlessly and heatedly. It was enjoyable. I lost track of Joe when we went into action in Italy. A month later I was hit at Luciana. Then Joe was killed while on night patrol along the Arno River. I wouldn't believe it for a long time.

Ox and I met at a PX in Camp Shelby. He had on a raincoat that was buttoned fully to the neck. It was a warm night with not a cloud in the sky. I asked Ox what the raincoat was all about. "Beer," he says. "After the sixth bottle, I get sloppy and I don't want to get my uniform messed up." This guy has got to be some kind of boy scout; he comes prepared. By his fifth beer and my third, his raincoat has done its duty and he's telling me where the army can shove the short-order drills and the ten-mile hikes. I agree with him even without a raincoat.

Ox later became acting 1st Sgt of I Company during the Gothic Line action. He was killed by friendly artillery fire just after the breakthrough of the Gothic line.

Prisoners and guard wear smiles, no more fighting

Peace at Last

The swastika falls and I Company helps it to come down

For the men of the 100/442, the announcement of peace was a quiet moment, a good moment, a sad moment. There was no great cheering or frenzied jubilation. There was joy but of a quiet kind — joy that the killing would now end, joy that the maiming would now cease. There was no holding back the memories, or the tears for the ones who didn't make it or for the ones physically and mentally torn. There was restrained rejoicing in a victory hard-earned at bitter cost. The war was still too close. It had been too long. Many of them had been in combat for 20 months, in the thick of action, at the cutting edge. The 100th Infantry Battalion had fought with the 34th Division for 9 months. The Combat Team with the 100th as its first battalion had fought against the enemy for 11 months.

Six hundred and eighty men had been killed in action, 67 were missing, and 9,486 had been awarded Purple Hearts. This was the price the 100/442 had to pay.

Above, convoy moving troops out of Novi Liguri. A bath, a clean uniform, and a ride through the peaceful Italian countryside can produce miracles — note the smiles on the infantrymen's faces. Left, the cessation of hostilities produces many amenities. Note, one, the hot food. Note, two, the use of messkits instead of shovels for plates. Note, finally, the comfortable dinner ensemble the men are wearing. Left to right — T/4 George Katada, S/Sgt Isaac Ikehara, and PFC Toichi Doi, K Company, 3d Bn

143

• *Fellas, the war which we fought, the war in which all our friends who slept with us and ate with us died, who wanted to see this day. The war is over. You know, not one man cheered. I think most of them cried, I mean, just thinking of their friends that wanted to see this day. I mean, you see people in New York having all kinds of, man, just cheering. I just couldn't see that, you know. The guys that went to the line, there was not one exhibition of cheering or jumping or anything. They just stood there at attention. You could see tears rolling down their eyes; I can't forget things like that you know. They, uh . . . to me, they never forgot the guys that lived with them and wanted to see that day, too.*

Left, a typical liberation day scene — wild and woolly. Carrara, Italy. Above, female collaborators get a haircut; male collaborators got worse, they got shot

Left, the war is over for both friend and foe. Here, at Ghedi airport, a prisoner of war (POW) camp was temporarily and hastily set up. Above, Pvt George Masushige, Company C, and PFC Masao Iraha, Company D, sort materials obtained from POW's. Over 5,000 prisoners were cleared through Ghedi

Decorations
100th Infantry Battalion and the 442d Regimental Combat Team

     7 Major campaigns in Europe
     7 Presidential Unit Citations
 9,486 Casualties (Purple Hearts)
18,143 Individual decorations, including:
     1 Congressional Medal of Honor
    52 Distinguished Service Crosses
     1 Distinguished Service Medal
   560 Silver Stars, with 28 Oak Leaf Clusters in lieu of second
        Silver Star awards
    22 Legion of Merit Medals
 4,000 Bronze Stars, 1,200 Oak Leaf Clusters
        representing second Bronze Stars
    15 Soldier's Medals
    12 French Croix de Guerre, with two Palms representing second
        awards
     2 Italian Crosses for Military Merit
     2 Italian Medals for Military Valor

In addition to the individual awards earned, the Combat Team, as a unit, won 36 Army Commendations, 87 Division Commendations, Meritorious Service Plaques for the Medical Detachment and Service Company, and 7 Presidential Unit Citations. Five of these were earned in a one-month period during the fighting for Bruyeres and the "Lost Battalion." (The Presidential Unit Citation for a unit is deemed the equivalent of the Distinguished Service Cross for the individual.) Additional postwar honors included a tribute from Gen George C. Marshall, Chief of Staff, U.S. Army, in his report to Congress; a further tribute from Winston Churchill, Prime Minister of England, in his report to Parliament; and a presidential invitation to march down Pennsylvania Avenue and attend a reception at the White House to receive the Presidential Unit Citation.

Lt Gen John C.H. Lee with Col Virgil Miller (left) fastens the Presidential Unit Citation to the regimental standard. The color bearers all wear the Silver Star: left to right, T/Sgt George Nishimura, T/Sgt William Higashiyama, S/Sgt Kay Kobata, S/Sgt Takashi Ueno

• *The question has arisen whether those of alien parents, of alien cultures, of many nations, many races, white, black, brown, yellow, red, can really and truly be knit by a common idealism into a nation, whether they have entered into and really become part of the warp and woof of the pattern of our national life or whether they are merely a heterogeneous mass of clashing colors. You, William Anderson, Lawrence Murphy, William Kamaka, Shiro Togo, William Goo, George Bergstrom, Ernest Damkroger,* *Douglas McNair, Kyotoshi Watanabe, Alvin Wong, Ralph Yang, Howard Vierra, and all others listed on this monument have answered that question. Your deaths should silence for all time those preaching racial intolerance — should forever still the tongues of discord that would divide our people.*

Your heroic sacrifice is not lost, but will mold and inspire the characters of generations yet unborn. INGRAM M. STAINBACK
GOVERNOR OF HAWAII

A memorial service in honor of their fallen comrades was held by the special companies of the Fifth Army's 442d Japanese American Combat Team on May 6, 1945, at Novi Liguri, near Genoa, Italy.

Beneath a warm Italian sun, in a setting of green countryside rich with the promise of new life and hope, the living pledged themselves to carry on the fight for which their fallen comrades had given their lives.

An altar was arranged beneath a flowering chestnut tree. It was draped with the blue flag and white cross of the church. Across it lay a row of red roses.

The simple ceremony opened with the playing of a musical prelude by the 206th Army Ground Forces Band of the 442d. An invocation was given by Captain Michael A.S. Yost of Nazareth, Pennsylvania, chaplain of the 100th Battalion of the 442d Combat Team.

The men, standing bare-headed, joined him in repeating the Lord's Prayer and in singing the hymn, "Rock of Ages."

Chaplain Yost then offered a prayer for the dead, and placed upon the living the duty of carrying on the work for a universal and lasting peace for which their comrades had sacrificed their lives.

Following a Scripture reading by Captain Hiro Higuchi of Pearl City, Hawaii, chaplain of 2d Battalion, Captain Masao Yamada of Kealakekua, Hawaii, chaplain of the 3d Battalion, offered a meditation.

After the singing of "God Bless America," Lieutenant Colonel James M. Hanley of Mandan, North Dakota, executive officer of the 442d introduced Colonel Virgil R. Miller of Winneconne, Wisconsin, commanding officer of the Combat Team.

In his address, Colonel Miller praised the veteran fighters of his command for the reputation they had achieved as one of the best American assault units in Europe.

"The sacrifice made by our comrades was great," he said. "We must not fail them in the fight that continues, in the fight that will be with us even when peace comes. Your task will be the harder and more arduous one, for it will extend over a longer time."

He warned his men against expecting too much upon their return home. "There will be more than eleven million returning veterans," he pointed out. "But the splendid record you have made, at great sacrifice by you and your fallen comrades, will aid you immeasurably in finding your places in the postwar world."

The men bent their heads in misty-eyed silence as Chaplain Yost read the Honor Roll of the dead. Two bugles played taps, one in soft echo of the other. Chaplain Yost pronounced a benediction.

The ceremony was concluded with the singing of "The Star Spangled Banner."

Spit-and-Polish

After the surrender of the German Army in Italy on May 2, the 100/442 was pulled back to the Novi Liguri bivouac area. Here they were metamorphosed from grubby, unwashed, and unshaven dogfaces into spit-and-polish garrison soldiers. This was tough. They even had to learn to salute again. At the front, the officers didn't want to be saluted — it was a signal for a sniper to pick them off. Now that everything was rear echelon, most of the guys had to salute anything that moved. It was also a time for re-education; for example, those funny looking overseas GI dollars were not cigar store coupons. They

Left, it's that "gangbusting" squad from the 3d Platoon of G Company. S/Sgt Dave Ito, 2d Squad Leader, is at extreme left, Ghedi Airport, Italy. Above, PFC Bob Nakamura, Oahu, Hawaii, drapes his laundry on a line strung from the wire-cutter bar on the front end of the jeep to the ammo can. Right, neither a thousand enemy troops nor ten thousand enemy shells could stay this charging convoy but Mother Nature did

were real money and should be pocketed for safekeeping. After all, you now had a good chance of coming out of the war alive. And here comes the brass. It was time for more decorations. On May 13 an impressive parade and ceremony were reviewed at the Novi Liguri airport by Lt Gen Lucian K. Truscott, Commanding General of the 5th Army, and by Maj Gen Edward M. Almond, Commanding General of the 92d Infantry Division.

The fighting had come to an end. But now the tidying up began. The Germans, with their weapons and supplies, were scattered over the width and breadth of northern Italy. Thousands were surrendering daily. The

The Combat Team's 206th Army Ground Forces Band plays at a ceremony in Italy

care-and-feeding, the processing-and-guarding of prisoners became the chore of Allied troops, the 100/442 included. On May 16, the Combat Team moved 125 miles northeast from Novi Liguri to Ghedi Airport near Brescia. There they processed, debugged, and guarded some 5,000 prisoners. On June 14, the 100/442 was relieved from the airport guard duty, and moved to Lecco some 60 miles closer to the beautiful lake country of Italy. The 206th Army Ground Forces Band was attached to IV Corps, and the 232d Combat Engineers left for an assignment in Florence. The 522d Field Artillery Battalion had already been severed and was serving in Central France, Austria, and Germany as road and checkpoint guards.

Above, the 3d Bn of the 100/442 takes on the orphans of Pisa. In this encounter, they lost their hearts. Top right, F Company's Melvin Tsuchiya is Santa Claus. Hank Oyasoto and Kiyo Morimoto (right) are his helpers. Right, G Company waves a fond farewell to a truckload of orphans after their Christmas party, December 25, 1945

Rest and Recreation, Army Style

After a month of guarding thousands of POW's on a hot, dusty field, the men welcomed the cool, lovely environs of Lecco, the vacation area of the Italians. Rest, recreation and sports filled the schedule. But on June 19, the 100/442 was redesignated as a Category II unit subject to transfer to the Pacific Theater. So after just five days of rest, recreation and you-name-it, the battle-tested men had to undergo yet another full-fledged training routine. And they trained until 7 July, when they were abruptly transferred to the Pisa-Livorno-Firenze area. There,

Above, one year after liberation, the 100/442 parade in armored halftracks in Carrara, Italy. Right, will wonders never cease, infantrymen of the 100/442 riding again, this time in an armored car sprouting a 37mm anti-tank gun

Above, the 100/442 passes in review in Leghorn, Italy. It was a time for ceremony and decorations — then back to the "trenches." Below, K Company marches by and gives a salute to the colors by the officers with an "eyes right" by the men. Band plays in the background. Far right, the 100/442 Regimental Combat Team in full review with guidons and colors.

their job was to guard German POW units and installations, and to supervise POW work duties. But all was not work. The men finally got the opportunity to go on leave to Switzerland, Greece, and the "lake country" of northern Italy. They were also able to attend schools and universities, and to participate in sports and athletic events. During the summer, 194 men and 4 officers with sufficient command of the Japanese language volun-

teered for the Military Intelligence Service Language School and further service in the Pacific.

However, all requirement for further combat service came to an end with President Truman's proclamation of VJ Day on September 2, 1945. The war in the Pacific was over. Peace reigned everywhere. It was glorious. To celebrate VJ Day, the 100/442 marched at the head of 15,000 Allied troops through the city of Livorno, Italy.

The end of the war marked the beginning of civilian life for many of the combat veterans of the 100/442. On the basis of an elaborate point system based on overseas service, decorations, and other factors, the veterans were allowed to return home. Although the 100/442 remained as occupation troops for over a year, by 1946 the veterans had been all but replaced by new troops. They had gone home to Hawaii or to the mainland to resume life as civilians.

Left, Lt Gen John C. H. Lee salutes the colors of the 100/442 at an awards ceremony in Leghorn, Italy, June 1946. Above, T/4 Wilfred Taira, Medic, Honolulu, receives the Bronze Star from Col Joseph Loef, October 1945. Top right, Lt Gen Lucian Truscott with Col Virgil Miller (right) salutes L Company after tying the Presidential Unit Citation to the guidon. Bottom right, Lt Gen Truscott attaches yet another Presidential Unit Citation ribbon to the 3d Bn guidon. All awards were made in Leghorn, Italy

July 4, 1946, Camp Kilmer, N.J., amputees wear leis (flown in from Hawaii) to greet returning veterans of the 100/442

● *Well, they were received as heroes by their own people, naturally, and I think that the general public received them as such now. There are a few cases, and I know that people would yell that they did not win the war. And I have got to give the men credit and the officers that are coming back and the spokesman for them, because this was mentioned on many occasions, that they did not win the war, that they fought as well as any soldier perhaps, not any better, but we knew of none that fought better. And I think it was this sort of humbleness that kept it in the right perspective so that people have accepted it very well.*

COL JAMES LOVELL
100th INFANTRY BATTALION

● *The Nisei bought an awful big hunk of America with their blood. We cannot let a single injury to be done them without defeating the purposes for which they fought.*

GENERAL JOSEPH W. STILWELL

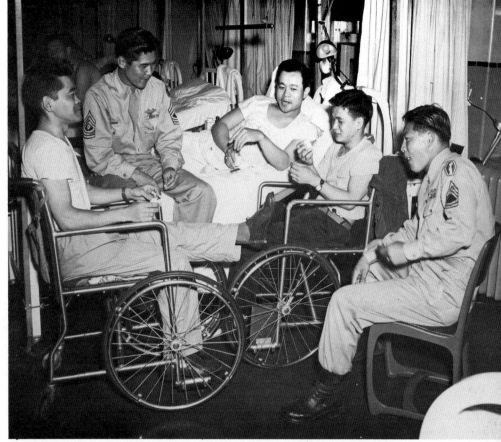

Left, impromptu string ensemble serenades the wounded at an army hospital with Hawaiian song (note electric guitar, right, a novelty then). Above, left to right, Wilson Makabe, 1st Sgt Tom Harimoto, Frank Fujino, Terumi Kato, and T/Sgt George Miki feasting on "manju" (sweet bean confection), Walter Reed General Hospital, 1946

To the Victor Belongs?

The returning Hawaiian veterans, Americans of Japanese ancestry, were greeted with open arms by the entire community. In Hawaii, they were members of the dominant minority — 160,000 out of a total population of 400,000. The Nisei and the Issei were employed, were visible, and received favorable media reports. During the war, newspaper reports and radio commentaries had been sympathetic to the 100/442 GI. As the war came to an end, favorable news of the exploits of the Combat Team became even more common. Also, on the Hawaiian homefront, a considerable number of Japanese Americans had conspicuous opportunity to demonstrate their

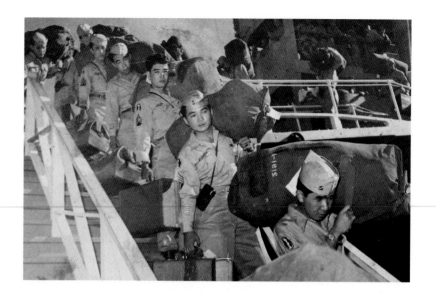

Top left, men of the 100/442 debarking in Honolulu from the Waterbury Victory. Left, Hoboken, N.J., reception committee awaiting veterans of the 100/442. Above, troop ship, Wilson Victory, transporting members of the 100/442 back to the states, 1946

These are the first 48 veterans of the 100/442 to be discharged from the Army. All but two were members of the battle-hardened 100th Infantry Battalion that saw service in Southern Italy with the 34th Division before teaming up with the 442

loyalty. They worked in civil defense, they built military installations, they bought gobs of war bonds, and they served in the Red Cross.

Although many of the mainland Japanese Americans did likewise when they could, often times it went unnoticed. They were a tiny minority — less than 1% — of the mainland population. Even worse, they had been removed and unable to return to the area where their visible evidences of loyalty and devotion would have counted the most, the West Coast.

On the mainland, the Japanese Americans returning to the West Coast received a somewhat different homecoming. Night riders warned Mary Masuda — the sister of S/Sgt Kazuo Masuda, who had earned a Distinguished Service Cross posthumously — not to return to her home. A barber in a small town just outside San Francisco refused to give a haircut to Capt Daniel Inouye, whose chest was bedecked with many decorations, and whose empty right sleeve gave eloquent testimony that an arm had been given in service to his coun-

164

try. PFC Wilson Makabe, seriously wounded on patrol in the Arno River sector — losing his right leg in a mortar blast — called his brother from the hospital to learn that their home had mysteriously burned to the ground when they attempted to return. PFC Richard Naito, wounded and disabled, applied for membership in the local Veterans of Foreign Wars (VFW) post only to be turned down and told to "go join his own." These are just a few of the many incidents that happened to the veterans returning to the mainland. Most of these incidents occurred on the West Coast.

But now the tables began to turn. Comrades in arms

The yacht, Lady Joe, greets Hawaii vets aboard the Waterbury Victory

PFC Marshall Higa, original 100th, was among the first to go home

Veterans of battles in Italy and France await discharge

It is my sincerest hope that America shall not burden any other ethnic group with the terrible dilemma forced on many Japanese Americans a scant four decades ago: whether to remain with their loved ones or leave them to an uncertain fate to help defend the nation responsible for their incarceration. So many paid with their blood to demonstrate their loyalty, yet died with the uncertainty that their children might be considered less American than other citizens.

SENATOR DANIEL K. INOUYE

Above, I Company men celebrate a family gathering. Right, during a more somber occasion, Mrs. Hana Harada receives the Silver Star

medal awarded posthumously to her son, Sgt Charles Harada. Presentation was made by Chaplain (Col) Corwin Olds, 1945

• *I would say that overall there was a hastening of the political, economic, social level of the Japanese people of Hawaii because of the war, because of the performance of the 100th and the 442d in the war. I guess all of these things would have happened without the war, but I think it would have been a slower process, that you had to overcome all of these obstacles of being immigrants and not being educated, not having the cultural background. You had to overcome these things in other ways, but because of the war, we hurried up this process.*

• *I am proud that I am an American citizen of Japanese ancestry, for my very background makes me appreciate more fully the wonderful advantages of this Nation.*

I believe in her institutions, ideals and traditions; I glory in her heritage; I boast of her history; I trust in her future.

Because I believe in America, and I trust she believes in me, and because I have received innumerable benefits from her, I pledge myself to do honor to her at all times and in all places.

JAPANESE AMERICAN CREED 1942
MIKE MASAOKA

● *If we the living, the beneficiaries of their sacrifices are truly intent upon showing our gratitude, we must do more than gather together for speechmaking and perfunctory ceremonies. We must undertake to carry on the unfinished work which they so nobly advanced. The fight against prejudice is not confined to the battlefield, alone. It is still here and with us now. So long as a single member of our citizenry is denied the use of public facilities and denied the right to earn a decent living because, and solely because of the color of his skin, we who 'fought against prejudice and won' ought not sit idly by and tolerate the perpetuation of injustices . . .*

SENATOR SPARK M. MATSUNAGA

Top left, the way it was — home again with the family. Far left, Sgt Hisashi Nakashima receives a tearful but joyous welcome home, Honolulu. Left, PFC Harry Iwafuchi and wife, Arline, are rejoined at long last, San Francisco. Above, Sgt Robert Katayama is embraced by his father, Honolulu

167

from the different units that they had served with in Europe came to the rescue of the beleaguered "battalion" of Japanese Americans. Also, a large and growing number of fair-play and fair-minded Americans began to intercede on behalf of the Japanese Americans.

President (then Captain) Ronald Reagan and Gen "Vinegar Joe" Stilwell joined forces with Mary Masuda and her family. At a ceremony awarding the Distinguished Service Cross posthumously to S/Sgt Masuda, Capt Reagan declared, "Blood that has soaked into the sands of a beach is all one color. America stands unique in the world, the only country not founded on race, but on a way — an ideal." Gen Stilwell presented Mary with her brother's award in recognition of her own courage in defying the night riders. Gen Stilwell, outraged at the night riders, said, "We ought to take a pick-ax handle

Above, Earl Finch, center, was host and mentor to countless Nisei GI's during their training days at Camp Shelby, Hattiesburg, Mississippi. Their loyalty at that time was in question and they had yet to prove themselves in battle, yet Earl Finch extended his hand of friendship without strings and without reservation. Here, after the war, this act of brotherhood was not forgotten. His many friends joined him at many such reunions — now wearing the ribbons and awards of battle-tested soldiers; they joined in a salute to the man who symbolized America at her finest

The Japanese American soldiers, though repressed in this country at a period in history less enlightened than our own, valiantly fought to preserve the ideals of freedom proclaimed by that country. No man, no group could have done more. In retrospect, we clearly see that many of our past deeds have been colored by emotion, prejudice or unfounded fear toward our fellow men or our countrymen. I would like to believe that those actions exhibited the attitude of the times and were attitudes which we, as a nation, have long since outgrown. And that now we are forever the wiser. But, though we may have a long way to go in this direction of human understanding, I am nonetheless very proud of our nation and our people because we possess that rare and unique humility and compassion to admit past faults, seek corrections, and make amends . . . this quality is rare on this earth. And even today, it is one of the privileges and blessings worth fighting for to preserve. Thank you for your unparalleled heroism which shall always remain an inspiration for all Americans.

BRIG GEN ROBERT F. YOUNG
CHIEF OF STAFF, SIXTH U.S. ARMY

A good democracy is made of good people that wish to cooperate with each other; not by outside force but by inner discipline of the spirit and goodwill toward our neighbors, which is Peace's only safeguard. That is the strongest test of manners and morals that democracy must solve. We have won the war against fascism abroad, but that is not our whole duty. We must sacrifice selfishness for the larger interest of society and courageously live the principles of tolerance and fair play in our daily lives in contact with our neighbors.

MARY MASUDA
(SISTER OF S/SGT KAZUO MASUDA, DSC, KIA)

after such people." Upon receiving the honor, Mary gave the medal to her mother.

Col Virgil Miller, commander of the 100/442 Regimental Combat Team, took the VFW to task with a scathing denunciation of the local post's membership policies (re PFC Naito) and of the officers who backed them. The president of the national VFW agreed with Col Miller, censured the post and labelled their action "stupid." Today, the VFW, locally and nationally, is one of the staunchest supporters of veterans of all races and creeds.

PFC Makabe and Capt Inouye, unfortunately, received no such vindication or satisfaction.

But, in general, the veterans' faith that fair play and the democratic process would prevail proved to be prophetic. Within ten years, the walls of discrimination against the Japanese Americans in particular and minority groups everywhere began to crumble. Down came the Alien Land Law, the Oriental Exclusion Act (barring immigration), the anti-naturalization laws, the miscegenation laws, and a teetering pile of state and municipal statutes which denied the Asian American the same rights and privileges his counterpart from Europe had enjoyed for years.

Bottom left, monument dedicated to the soldiers of the 100/442 by the town of Bruyeres, France. Above, Gen Mark W. Clark holds son of T/4 Yom Nosei during a decoration ceremony. Yom's mother is flanked by Gen Clark and Lt Gen John E. Hull, Hawaii, 1948

● *In the '50s, Hollywood made a full-length, feature film of the 100/442 entitled, "Go For Broke," starring Van Johnson, with supporting roles by actual members of the unit, Henry Oyasato, Sunshine Fukunaga, George Miki, Tom Aikens, and technical advisor, Mike Masaoka.*

Some 30 years later, on March 7, 1981, to a standing-room-only assembly of over 2000 persons, the Presidio Army Museum, San Francisco, formally dedicated an exhibit honoring the 100th Infantry Battalion and the 442d Regimental Combat Team. The ceremony consisted of: a 17-gun salute; troops in review; addresses by Senators Daniel Inouye and Spark Matsunaga; Mayor (San Francisco) Dianne Feinstein; Chief of Staff, U.S. 6th Army, Gen Robert Young; Post Commander, Col Whitney Hall, Jr.; Curator, the Presidio Army Museum, Eric Saul; and JACL "elder statesman," Mike Masaoka. A heartfelt rendition of "God Bless America" by the Watsonville Japanese American Senior Citizens Choir (Issei, ages 72 to 95), many of whom had sons in the 100/442 — two were Gold Star mothers — reaffirmed the loyalty and devotion to the United States that both they and the Nisei had so steadfastly displayed both on the homefront and on the battlefront.

169

Keep Up the Fight

The courage and faith shown by the men of the 100/442 were honored by an exhibit at the Presidio Army Museum in San Francisco in 1981. At the dedication ceremony, Senator Spark Matsunaga said, "In the sacrifices made by the veterans of the 100/442d Regimental Combat Team, in their courage and loyalty, we can find strength and determination to continue our seemingly endless battle against discrimination and injustice . . . to make ours a greater nation in a better world."

On the same occasion, Senator Daniel Inouye asked, "Does anyone truly believe Hawaii would have become a state in 1959 if the 100/442 had not been formed; if Japanese Americans remained satisfied with their 4-C Selective Service status? Do you think the Oriental Exclusion Act that had established race as a barrier to naturalization and immigration would have been repealed if so many of our friends and loved ones had not served and died so bravely? Perhaps it would have come about eventually, but the wait would certainly have been a long one . . . I would like to believe that our wartime sacrifice had something to do with the extension of civil rights and dignity, not only to Japanese Americans, but to all citizens of this nation."

That plain-speaking man from Middle America probably summed it up best in 1946 when he presented the final Presidential Unit Citation to the 100/442d Regi-

Left, 100/442 Regimental Combat Team marching down Pennsylvania Avenue to the White House to receive the Presidential Unit Citation from President Harry S. Truman. Above, President Truman and Lt

Col Alfred S. Pursall, Commanding Officer, 3d Bn, 100/442 salute the colors prior to the presentation of the seventh Presidential Unit Citation

mental Combat Team. At the presentation ceremony on the White House lawn, President Harry S. Truman stated, "You fought for the free nations of the world . . . you fought not only the enemy, you fought prejudice — and you won. Keep up that fight . . . continue to win — make this great Republic stand for what the Constitution says it stands for: 'the welfare of all the people, all the time.' "

● *There is one supreme, final test of loyalty for one's native land — readiness and willingness to fight for, and if need be, to die for one's country. These Americans pass that test with colors flying. They proved their loyalty and devotion beyond all question.*

They volunteered for Army combat service and they made a record second to none. In Europe, theirs was the Combat Team most feared by the enemy. In the Pacific, they placed themselves in double jeopardy, chancing the bullets of friend as well as foe. Everywhere they were the soldiers most decorated for valor, most devoted to duty. Their only absences without leave were from hospitals which they quit before recovered from their wounds, in order to get back into the fight for what they knew to be right.

These men . . . more than earned the right to be called just Americans, not Japanese Americans. Their Americanism may be described only by degree, and that the highest.

MAJ GEN JACOB L. DEVERS
CHIEF OF THE ARMY FIELD FORCES

References

Ambassadors in Arms, by Thomas D. Murphy; *Americans: The Story of the 442d Combat Team,* by Orville C. Shirey; *America's Concentration Camps,* by Allan R. Bosworth; *The Bamboo People: The Law and Japanese Americans,* by Frank F. Chuman; *Beach Head News,* U.S. Army newspaper, articles; *The Boys from Company B,* by Richard S. Oguro; *Concentration Camps U.S.A.: Japanese Americans and World War II,* by Roger Daniels; *Congressional Record,* proceedings, debates, and articles of the 88th Congress; *Des Moines Register,* newspaper articles; *442d Combat Team,* by Orville C. Shirey, produced in Italy by MTOUSA (Mediterranean Theater of Operations, United States Army); *The Garden Island* newspaper, article by Ichiro Okada; *History of The 232d Engineer Combat Company,* by George Goto; *Japanese Americans and World War II,* by Donald Teruo Hata, Jr., and Nadine Ishitani Hata; *Japanese Americans: the Evolution of a Sub-culture,* by Harry Kitano; *Journey to Washington,* by Daniel K. Inouye, with Lawrence Elliott; *Nisei: The Pride and the Shame,* documentary film by CBS/TV, narrated by Walter Cronkite; *Nisei: The Quiet American,* by Bill Hosokawa; *Pacific Citizen,* newspaper published by JACL (Japanese American Citizens League), articles; *San Francisco Chronicle* newspaper, articles; *Soldiers,* the official magazine of the U.S. Army, November 1978, article; *These Are Americans,* by John D. Rademaker; *Unit Histories* of the 34th Division, the 36th Division, and the 92d Division; *Unit Journal — 100th Infantry Battalion (Separate); Wartime Hysteria: The Role of the Press,* by Florence Yoshiwara; *Yankee Samurai,* by Joseph D. Harrington; *Years of Infamy,* by Michi Weglyn; *Puka Puka Parade,* "Enemy Forces Facing the 100/442," preliminary report (1981), by Donald Shearer.

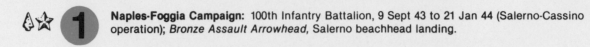 **Naples-Foggia Campaign:** 100th Infantry Battalion, 9 Sept 43 to 21 Jan 44 (Salerno-Cassino operation); *Bronze Assault Arrowhead,* Salerno beachhead landing.

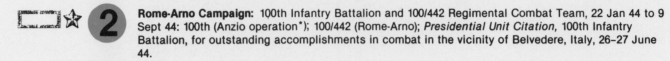 **Rome-Arno Campaign:** 100th Infantry Battalion and 100/442 Regimental Combat Team, 22 Jan 44 to 9 Sept 44: 100th (Anzio operation*); 100/442 (Rome-Arno); *Presidential Unit Citation,* 100th Infantry Battalion, for outstanding accomplishments in combat in the vicinity of Belvedere, Italy, 26–27 June 44.

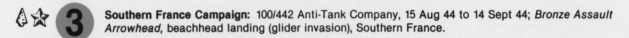 **Southern France Campaign:** 100/442 Anti-Tank Company, 15 Aug 44 to 14 Sept 44; *Bronze Assault Arrowhead,* beachhead landing (glider invasion), Southern France.

 **Northern Apennines Campaign:** 100/442 Regimental Combat Team, 10 Sept 44 to 4 April 45.

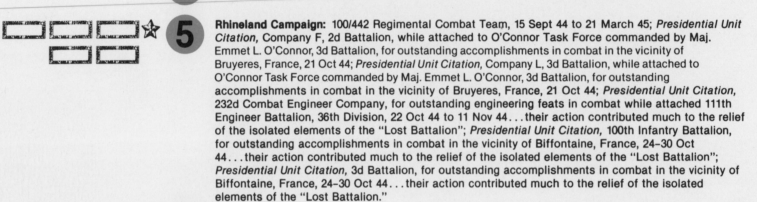 **Rhineland Campaign:** 100/442 Regimental Combat Team, 15 Sept 44 to 21 March 45; *Presidential Unit Citation,* Company F, 2d Battalion, while attached to O'Connor Task Force commanded by Maj. Emmet L. O'Connor, 3d Battalion, for outstanding accomplishments in combat in the vicinity of Bruyeres, France, 21 Oct 44; *Presidential Unit Citation,* Company L, 3d Battalion, while attached to O'Connor Task Force commanded by Maj. Emmet L. O'Connor, 3d Battalion, for outstanding accomplishments in combat in the vicinity of Bruyeres, France, 21 Oct 44; *Presidential Unit Citation,* 232d Combat Engineer Company, for outstanding engineering feats in combat while attached 111th Engineer Battalion, 36th Division, 22 Oct 44 to 11 Nov 44...their action contributed much to the relief of the isolated elements of the "Lost Battalion"; *Presidential Unit Citation,* 100th Infantry Battalion, for outstanding accomplishments in combat in the vicinity of Biffontaine, France, 24–30 Oct 44...their action contributed much to the relief of the isolated elements of the "Lost Battalion"; *Presidential Unit Citation,* 3d Battalion, for outstanding accomplishments in combat in the vicinity of Biffontaine, France, 24–30 Oct 44...their action contributed much to the relief of the isolated elements of the "Lost Battalion."

 **Central Europe Campaign:** 522d Field Artillery Battalion, 22 Mar 45 to 11 May 45.

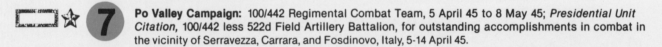 **Po Valley Campaign:** 100/442 Regimental Combat Team, 5 April 45 to 8 May 45; *Presidential Unit Citation,* 100/442 less 522d Field Artillery Battalion, for outstanding accomplishments in combat in the vicinity of Serravezza, Carrara, and Fosdinovo, Italy, 5-14 April 45.

---

* As we go to press, correspondence from the Department of the Army, Chief of Military History, accords the Anzio action the status of a "Campaign" (making it the eighth for the 100/442 RCT). The same letter records the 100th Battalion as having received the Presidential Unit Citation for the Gothic Line action. This would raise the total of Presidential Unit Citations won by the 100/442 RCT to an unprecedented eight. Further verification is pending.

LEGEND: —Bronze Battle Star for each campaign

—Bronze Arrowhead for participation in amphibious or airborne landing on hostile shores.

— Presidential Unit Citation: awarded to units by the President of the United States for extraordinary heroism in combat.